THE BOY SCOUT ENCYCLOPEDIA

Songs around the campfire end a perfect day

THE
BOY SCOUT
ENCYCLOPEDIA

Text and illustrations prepared
under the direction of
THE BOY SCOUTS OF AMERICA

Text by **BRUCE GRANT**

Illustrations by **FIORE and JACKIE MASTRI**

RAND McNALLY & COMPANY
New York   CHICAGO   San Francisco

LIBRARY OF CONGRESS CATALOG CARD NUMBER: 52-10413

A WORD ABOUT THIS BOOK

TO the boys of America we offer in this book a new kind of adventure. Here you will find a panorama of Scouting. Here are presented the skills of the Boy Scout, the wisdom of the woods, the craft of the Indian, pioneer lore from the western frontiers, and the color, the drama, and the zest that make Scouting the greatest game for boys on earth.

Here, too, you will find something of the fun and the achievements that Cub Scouts enjoy; also activities with the tang of the sea and inland waters, aviation know-how, and wilderness expeditions that challenge Explorers.

Whatever your age, whether you are in Scouting or not, we have tried to bring you rich entertainment of the sort that appeals to red-blooded young Americans.

The material for these articles has been carefully selected from many different sources. Mr. Bruce Grant has done a splendid job in developing the text, and the lively illustrations of Fiore and Jackie Mastri enhance its value. Expert Scouters have carefully reviewed the material so that you may rely on the accuracy of what you find here. THE BOY SCOUT ENCYCLOPEDIA is not intended to be a basic handbook, but to present a panorama of the Scout program as it is carried on by millions of boys throughout the United States and, indeed, the world.

As those in Scouting know, the activities of the Scout program have been developed to help boys grow into sturdy, self-reliant, unselfish citizens. We hope that these pages may help to impress upon you the deep spiritual values of the Scout Oath and Law and the ideals of Scouting.

In this connection I would like to tell you of an incident which occurred at the Seventh World Jamboree, which was held in Austria. A Scout World Jamboree is a great camp of representatives of all the Scout organizations in the world. On this particular evening our Scouts had each invited a foreign Scout friend to sit with him at our campfire. Picture the scene. A campfire amongst the mountains, thousands of boys, and upon a distant peak an illuminated cross standing out from the top of the mountain. Over all shone the full moon, God's creation, and there below were boys of all faiths and all nationalities, the destiny of the world.

They conducted a candlelight ceremony. Each American Scout had a candle, and broke his candle and gave half of it to a Scout from another country as a sign of world brotherhood. What a thrill as all over the mountainside you could see the candles light up and the Scouts of sixty free nations of the world solemnly pledge "On their Honor" to do their duty to God, to help other people at all times, and to obey the Scout Law.

When it was over one boy came to me and asked for my autograph, saying, "Chief, I want you to write something in my book that will live with me the rest of my life." I took my pen and wrote: "May the candlelight of this ceremony ever burn in your heart and mine, reminding both of us of our responsibilities to serve our fellow man, our country, and our God."

So to those boys who use this book, I express the hope that it will serve as a challenge and an inspiration, so that you may be better trained "On your honor to do your best to do your duty to God and your Country."

ARTHUR A. SCHUCK
Chief Scout Executive

New York, N. Y.
July 14, 1952

THE BOY SCOUT ENCYCLOPEDIA

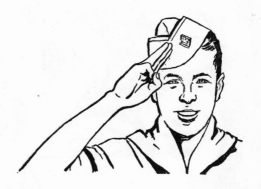

A Bicycle Patrol sets up camp for a week end in the woods

Ace Air Explorer. The highest rank in the Air Explorers, attained by qualifying in such skills as weather, airman, builder, navigation, communications, and mechanic and by putting into practice in daily life the Scout Oath and Law and Scout ideals of service and leadership. See Air Explorer, Scout Oath and Law.

Advancement. A Scout advances from Tenderfoot to Eagle rank by DOING THINGS with his Patrol and Troop. He learns skills, such as making a fire, cooking a meal, or pitching a tent. These are a part of the adventure of Scouting, to help him become a better hiker and camper and a better citizen of his community and country.

The requirements for all ranks are divided into three parts—Scout Spirit, Scout Participation, and Scoutcraft. Scout Spirit means how well he lives the life of a real Scout, true to his Scout Oath and Law.

For his Scout Participation he does his share in his Patrol and Troop, at home and in his community.

Scoutcraft he learns from his Patrol Leader, Scoutmaster, and other leaders, and by doing things himself. He practices such skills as stalking, sending a message in code, using the compass. He goes hiking and camping and does these things in the woods until he can prove to his leaders that he can do them well and is ready to advance to another rank.

The Scout then reports to a group of men, usually connected with his Troop, called a Board of Review. They talk over what he has done and ask him questions to make sure he is ready to advance.

The last part of the Scout's advancement takes place at a Court of Honor when he formally receives his new badge of rank while his parents and friends look on.

Cub Scouts and Explorers advance in rank in the same general way. See Board oe Review, Court of Honor.

Adventure Hike. See Hikes (Kinds of).

Advisor. The leader of an Explorer Unit. See Explorer, Explorer Advisor.

Aide, Scout. An outstanding Scout selected for his service record and assigned to a distinguished local guest to assist him, or to help delegates at a Local Council annual meeting or other formal occasion.

Air Explorer. The young man who wants to become a flier, or to learn air navigation, airplane design, or mechanics, can start at the age of fourteen. He can join the Air Explorers, a branch of the Explorer program for older Scouts, and learn the basic principles of aviation and even fly under an experienced leader.

The Air Explorer knows many skills

Air Explorers are organized in Crews. Two or more Crews make a Squadron of from five to thirty-two Air Explorers. The uniform is horizon blue. Ranks go from Apprentice, Observer, Craftsman, to Ace, the highest. Requirements include knowledge of airplane construction, weather, communications, navigation, hiking, and camping.

There are ratings which can be earned for special work. Explorers in Troops and Posts may work for aviation ratings. Activities include indoor, outdoor, social, and service projects. See EXPLORER.

Akela (a-kay'-lah). Cub Scout name for a good leader, such as Cubmaster, Den Mother, Den Chief, or parent. In Cub Scout Indian lore, Akela was Chief of the Webelos Tribe. He was a good and mighty Indian. "The Cub Scout follows Akela" is the first part of the Law of the Pack. See CUB SCOUT, WEBELOS.

American's Creed. Love of his country, support of its Constitution, obedience to its laws, respect for its Flag, and readiness to help defend it against all enemies are essential to the Boy Scout's character.

The Boy Scout finds his inspiration in the American's Creed, which was written in 1917 by William Tyler Page and accepted on behalf of the American people April 3, 1918, by the House of Representatives. The Creed is:

"I believe in the United States of America as a government of the people, by the people, for the people; whose just powers are derived from the consent of the governed; a democracy in a republic; a sovereign nation of many sovereign states; a perfect union, one and inseparable; established upon those principles of freedom, equality, justice, and humanity for which American patriots sacrificed their lives and fortunes.

"I therefore believe it is my duty to my country to love it; to support its constitution; to obey its laws; to respect its flag, and to defend it against all enemies." See CITIZENSHIP, SCOUT OATH AND LAW.

Animals. All living things other than plants. The Boy Scout studies animals and learns many valuable things from them. See BIRDS, INSECTS, MAMMALS, REPTILES.

Animal Signs. See TRACKS (ANIMAL).

Appalachian Trail. A mountain trail favored by older Scouts and Explorers. This trail runs from the peak of the mighty Katahdin in Maine to Mount Oglethorpe in Georgia. It passes through many state and national parks in the White Mountains, Green Mountains, Catskills, and Great Smokies, in all of which there are excellent camping sites. See EXPLORER.

Aquatics. See BOATS (Types), SAIL, SWIMMING.

Archery. The art or sport of shooting with a bow and arrow. Archery is popular with Scouts, especially in camp, where tournaments are often held. The Boy Scout

Archery is a popular sport in camp

learns to make his own bows, arrows, and equipment. He uses hickory, Osage orange, lemonwood, yew, and ash for bows. Arrows are harder to make. The Scout usually uses birch and learns to fletch, or put feathers on, his arrows. Scouts who earn the Merit Badge in archery are required to make their own equipment.

The Scout knows that the bow and arrow are third on the list of important things that have advanced mankind from cavemen. Only speech and the use of fire come ahead of them.

As the Scout shoots his Junior American Round to qualify for his Merit Badge, he may recall the glamorous days of Robin Hood and his merry men in Sherwood Forest, or the early Indian stalking his game in the deep forests, or the latter-day perfection of such archers and hunters as Maurice Thompson, who lived by the bow and arrow in the Florida Everglades, or of Howard Hill of movie fame.

Like other Scout activities, this sport gives to the Scout romance, skilled craftsmanship, expert performance, and fun. See ARROWHEADS, MERIT BADGES.

Arrowheads. Scout camp museums, Troop headquarters, and individual Scouts often have beautiful collections of arrowheads of all sizes and colors from gray flint to pink, green, pure white, and black stones that gleam like jewels.

In arrowhead country Scouts collect the arrowheads Indians made and lost long ago. Many Scouts, however, make their own arrowheads superbly, flaking and shaping them as the Indians did. They often "swap" arrowheads with one another to build up a collection of stones from all over the country. Arrowheads are also called arrowpoints.

1. War points   3. Hunting point
2. Bird point   4. Poison point

9

The Scout is trained and prepared to meet emergencies of many kinds

Artificial Respiration. The scene is on a beach unprotected by life guards. A man has just been pulled from the water. People crowd around excitedly. To all appearances the man is dead. No one seems to know what to do.

A boy pushes forward. In a calm, businesslike way he orders the crowd back. He requests someone to call a physician. Then he at once places the victim in the face-down prone position, bending his elbows and placing his hands one upon the other. He turns the man's face to one side so that his cheekbone rests upon his hands. He kneels at the head of the unconscious man with both hands flat on the victim's back. He exerts an even pressure downward, rocking forward at the same time. Then he rocks backward and draws the victim's arms upward.

"Must be a Boy Scout," someone says.

Yes, he is a Boy Scout. This is one of the many emergencies for which he is prepared, for which he has been well trained. He knows how to give artificial respiration— the back-pressure arm-lift method of artificial respiration—whereby good air is introduced into the lungs of a suffocated person and the bad air forced out. He knows how to give this first aid measure—how to save a life—when stoppage of breathing has resulted from being under water, from electric shock, mechanical strangulation, paralysis, being smothered or buried, or from other causes.

This knowledge and training enable the Boy Scout to render valuable service to his fellow-man, to save a life. He is a hero, but a modest hero. To him it is all in his day's services. Just another Good Turn. See "Be

10

PREPARED," FIRST AID, GOOD TURN, LIFE SAVING.

Assistant Scoutmaster. A Troop has one or more Assistant Scoutmasters. They help the Scoutmaster teach, lead games, run a camp, and take charge of the Troop, when necessary. They may be specialists in some activity, like first aid, outdoor skills, signaling.

Like the Scoutmaster, Assistants take training so as to be experts. An Assistant Scoutmaster has to be at least eighteen years of age and gets a commission, or written authority of leadership, from the National Council. Many Assistants were Scouts in the Troop they now serve as leaders. See JUNIOR ASSISTANT SCOUTMASTER, SCOUTMASTER, TROOP.

Associate Scout. A Scout or Explorer who, although he cannot attend Troop meetings regularly, registers with the Troop like other Scouts and promises to attend as many meetings as possible during the year, and to observe the Scout Oath and Law and the Daily Good Turn.

Athenian Oath. An oath taken around 300 B.C. by the boys of Athens when they reached the age of seventeen. The Boy Scout Code includes the ideals of the Athenian Oath. The Athenian Oath reads:

"We will never bring disgrace on this, our city, by an act of dishonesty or cowardice.

"We will fight for the ideals and Sacred Things of the city both alone and with many.

"We will revere and obey the city's laws, and will do our best to incite a like reverence and respect in those about us who are prone to annul them or set them at naught.

We will strive increasingly to quicken the public's sense of civic duty.

"Thus in all these ways we will transmit this city, not only not less, but greater, better, and more beautiful than it was transmitted to us." See CITIZENSHIP, SCOUT CODE.

Axe. An edged tool used for chopping, hewing, and many other purposes by the Scout. With the knife, it is one of the most important trail tools.

The Scout axe is the belt axe. This little axe, well balanced and easily carried, is an adaptation of the hatchet. It is light and sturdy and can be used to cut firewood, point a tent peg, make a bed, clear a trail, and build camp gadgets.

The Scout's belt axe is light and sturdy

The axe is a true friend of the Scout. And in turn, the Scout is the best friend of his axe. He keeps it shiny and sharp and uses it skillfully. He carries it in a sheath, perhaps made by himself. He knows the safety rules for carrying and passing his axe and his knife. "Safety through Skill" is a Scout slogan.

The Scout knows that if he carries his axe without a sheath, the edge should be turned outward from his side; if over the shoulder, the edge turned away from him. If he passes his axe to someone else, he passes it by the handle with the head down and the edge outward.

11

Back-Pack Expedition.   A real he-man hike requiring wilderness skill and physical stamina; especially an expedition by Explorers in which the back pack is used. See HIKES (KINDS OF), PACKS (FOR CARRYING).

Backwoods Scouting.   The test of the Scout, also termed backwoods engineering. The Scout uses the skills of the old pioneer woodsmen like Daniel Boone and Kit Carson, and such animals as the beaver, known as "the best backwoods engineer." With the help of his sharp axe, the Scout fells trees, splits firewood, builds bridges, makes shelters and rafts. See AXE, EXPLORER.

Back-Yard Camping.   An activity of Cub Scouts, in which they play at camping. Cub Scouts do not go on actual camping trips, but they can set up a tent in the back yard with Dad's help, roast potatoes or corn in hot coals with Mother's assistance, and make rustic furniture and play games. See CUB SCOUT.

Baden-Powell, Lord   (1857 - 1940). Founder of the world-wide Scout Movement. His title was Chief Scout of the World.

This brilliant and resourceful British officer conceived the idea of Scouting while training men in India and South Africa. He found the young men ill-fitted by city life

Lord Baden-Powell

to endure the hardships of outdoor living, and developed games and activities to make them strong and self-reliant under primitive conditions. During his courageous defense of Mafeking he demonstrated his ability to organize boys when he formed the youth of that city into a successful messenger corps.

Upon Baden-Powell's return to England, he was urged to adapt his training to boys. He began the study of boys' organizations, especially those of the two Americans, Dan

Beard and Ernest Thompson Seton, and out of these studies grew his plan for Boy Scouting.

"By the term Scouting," he said, "is meant the work and attributes of backwoodsmen, explorers, hunters, seamen, airmen, pioneers, and frontiersmen."

In 1907 Baden-Powell tried out his idea by taking twenty boys to a camp on Brownsea Island, off the coast of England. This first Boy Scout camp was a marked success, and the following year he organized the Boy Scouts and published his book, *Scouting for Boys.* See BEARD, BOY SCOUTS OF AMERICA.

Badge (Scout). See SCOUT BADGE.

Badges and Insignia. Emblems worn on the official uniform by all Scouts and denoting office, rank, and service as well as honors, decorations, and marks of distinction. The Scout takes pride in the badges and insignia on his uniform because they tell the world that he is qualified and can be relied upon to help people. Among the badges and insignia a Scout may wear

are the Patrol medallion, which is the Patrol totem; the Community strip, designating the home of the Troop; the Troop numeral; the badge of office, showing whether the Scout is a Patrol Leader, Bugler, or such; the badge of rank, designating whether the Scout is a Tenderfoot, Second Class Scout, and so on; the Webelos Badge, highest rank in Cub Scouting, and various badges, medals, and service stars. See EAGLE SCOUT, GOLD HONOR MEDAL, MERIT BADGES, SCOUT BADGE, UNIFORMS.

Balance of Nature. Two Scouts are hiking through a woods. One, an older boy, is an expert in wildlife and woodlore—he understands Nature. The other, younger, has had little outdoor experience.

"There should be squirrels around here," says the first Scout, kicking something on the ground. Sure enough, when they look up into the oak tree, they see the tiny head of a gray squirrel peeping around the upper part of the trunk.

"How did you know?" asks the second Scout.

"Oh, that was easy. There are acorns on

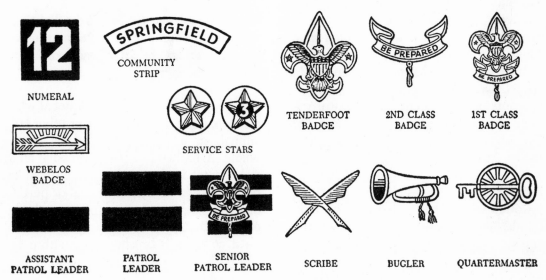

Badges and insignia show the Scout's rank and office

the ground. Squirrels like acorns—they live on them. So, naturally, where there are acorns there usually are squirrels."
bees."

"Sure!" exclaims the other. "You wouldn't have looked for squirrels if you had seen some clover blooming?"

"No, I probably would have looked for "And then we would look for honey!"

"Yep, and maybe where there was honey we could find some bears nearby. But I reckon the bears are all gone around here. But you see what I mean, don't you? In Nature almost everything has something to do with everything else. If we were to destroy these oak trees, the squirrels would leave. Other animals would leave, too. You see, all animals depend on plant life directly or indirectly for food. Look. You take the little plant lice that live on rosebushes, garden peas, and other plants. Ants or ladybird beetles eat the tiny lice. Flickers or robins eat the ants or beetles. Minks or hawks eat the robins or flickers. And that's the way it is—minks and hawks really have to depend on plant life. See?"

Thus two Scouts discuss the greatest of all wonders—Life. Or, better, what naturalists term the Balance of Nature. In her scheme Nature has a definite plan along which she works. Any conflict between Nature and Man happens because Man upsets that plan.

Scouts learn directly from Nature by close observation. See CONSERVATION, DESERT LIVING, EXPLORER, FORESTRY, GRASSLANDS, MARSHES, NATURE.

Bandaging. The binding or covering of a wound with a strip or band of soft cloth. Bandaging is usually an emergency action, and when a bandage is needed there is no time to experiment. The Scout must know just what to do. He must be prepared. There are many different kinds of bandages

for different types of wounds. Scouts know how to make and when to apply a triangle, a cravat, or a compression bandage.

Scouts carry first aid kits on all Scouting activities. They also know how to utilize materials at hand in an emergency. An emergency dressing can be made by tearing up a handkerchief, piece of shirttail, or other material and folding it into a small pad. But this must be sterilized, and the

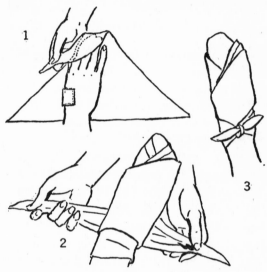

Steps in applying a hand bandage

Scout knows how to do this by lighting a match and scorching the material, thus killing the germs. See "BE PREPARED," FIRST AID.

Barbecue. An outdoor banquet at which a sheep, a pig, a side of beef or other large animal, or a fowl is broiled or roasted whole. A barbecue is an impressive affair. A huge pit is dug and a fire built at the bottom. Then the entire animal or portions of it are suspended on a spit over the hot coals of the fire and slowly turned. As the meat cooks, it is brushed over with a special barbecue sauce, usually made of vinegar, cooking oil, salt and pepper, and whatever other seasoning the cook wishes to add. The meat is served in large, juicy chunks. See IMU.

Barbecuing a pig

Bark Utensils. Scouts make emergency eating and cooking utensils such as kettles, plates, and cups from bark. The Scout finds the best barks are from dead white birch, elm, basswood, cottonwood, and poplar. See NATURE CRAFTS.

Beadwork. A popular handicraft, especially with Cub Scouts and in Scout camps. The beadwork of the North American Indian, with its beautiful colors and original designs, is used in ornamenting moccasins, belts, knife sheaths, neckerchief slides, and many other things. Boys learn appliqued or overlaid beading, attaching beads with the lazy stitch, or weaving them on looms. See INDIAN HANDICRAFT.

Bean-Hole Beans. Before Columbus came to these shores, many a Penobscot Indian smacked his lips at the thought of bean-hole beans. Now the Boy Scout makes this tasty dish in slightly modified form and he smacks his lips, too, at the thought of it. The recipe is to be found in the *Handbook for Boys* and the *Explorer Manual:*

Wash and soak 1½ pounds of dried lima or navy beans overnight. Boil until the bean skin splits when you blow on it. Drain. Then mix in ½ pound of salt pork cut in 1-inch cubes, 1 large onion chopped, 10 level tablespoons of brown sugar (or 6 level tablespoons of molasses), 1 level teaspoon dry mustard, 1 level teaspoon salt, and ¼ teaspoon of pepper. Pour in enough boiling water to cover, and secure the lid tightly.

Meantime the bean hole, lined with flat stones, has been heated with a fire burning in it until it is almost full of live coals. These coals are scooped out and the pot put in and covered with hot coals. The coals are then covered with earth. In from six to eight hours the beans are ready.

Bear Cub Scout. The third rank in Cub Scouting. See CUB SCOUT.

Beard, Daniel Carter ("Uncle Dan") (1850-1941). Author, artist, and naturalist and one of the most beloved men in Scouting. "Uncle Dan" was one of the organizers of the Boy Scouts of America, and from the beginning in 1910 until his death he served as National Scout Commissioner. In 1922 he was presented by his friends with a Gold Eagle Badge, the only one ever given. Beard also received the Roosevelt Gold Medal for Distinguished Service in 1927.

"Uncle Dan" helped found the Boy Scouts

In his early days Dan Beard made illustrations for many leading magazines, as well as popular books. He illustrated Mark Twain's *A Connecticut Yankee in King Arthur's Court.* He was an enthusiast of outdoor life and from 1905 to 1906 was editor of the magazine *Recreation*. He originated the "Sons of Daniel Boone" in 1901, a pioneer organization for boys, and wrote and illustrated many books for boys. See BADEN-POWELL, BOY SCOUTS OF AMERICA, NOGGIN.

Bell Time. A system of keeping time on shipboard to conform with the watches stood by the crew, each four hours in length. Each half hour is marked by the striking of a bell, the strokes being from one to eight. When more than one bell is struck, they are always given in pairs. Twelve o'clock, four o'clock, and eight o'clock are each "eight bells." See SEA EXPLORER.

"Be Prepared." A little girl's clothes were in flames. She had stepped too close to the small gas heater while dressing. She screamed, while her parents stood by

A Scout acts quickly and coolly

horror-stricken and the younger children cried in fright. Just then the brother, a Boy Scout, came running down the stairs. He snatched up a rug, rolled his sister in it,

and put out the flames before she was hurt.

"Thank God my son is a Scout," the father later told the Scoutmaster. "He knew what to do when we were all too frightened to act."

"He was prepared," replied the Scoutmaster.

This is a true story, one that happened in Oklahoma not so long ago.

"Be Prepared" is the Scout Motto. These words denote the Scout's spirit of serving—being ready always for an emergency.

The Scout is prepared to prevent accidents, to give first aid to the injured. Even to save a life. He is prepared to act in all kinds of disasters—fires, floods, earthquakes, and storms.

"Be prepared for what?" someone asked Baden-Powell, the founder of Scouting.

"Why, for any old thing," he replied.

The words "Be Prepared" are on the Scout Badge. See FIRST AID, GOLD HONOR MEDAL, SCOUT BADGE.

"Be Square." Part of the Cub Scout Promise. This means the Cub Scout will be fair and honest in all his dealings with people. See CUB SCOUT PROMISE AND LAW.

Bicycle Patrol. A Patrol in a Troop all of whose members have bicycles. They may take bicycle hikes and camp together as a Patrol. Often they are a part of the community's emergency defense program. Because they can move about quickly and are well trained, they help the local Red Cross and many other agencies in their work. There are not more than eight boys in a Bicycle Patrol.

Bird Feeders. Feeding of birds, especially during severe winter seasons, is an important project of Scouts. A Troop or Patrol may make a "nature trail" and label the shrubs and trees, telling what kinds of birds or mammals nest in or occupy them, or feed on them. The Scout also learns what birds live in a certain locality and their eating habits.

A suet box for winter feeding

In winter, feeding shelters for birds are supplied with suet and other meat fats, grains, and other vegetable food. The Scouts visit the feeders regularly and keep them filled. Scouts also plant food-bearing shrubs, sunflowers, and millet in food patches at their camps.

In placing feeding stations for birds, co-operation of the local game and forestry experts is obtained. See BIRD HIKING, BIRD-HOUSES, BIRDS, CONSERVATION, NATURE TRAIL.

Bird Hiking. An early-morning hike taken when the sun is not too high and birds can best be observed. Birds, after a night without food, feed at this time. In the heat of the day they are less active. The Scout looks for and observes birds of the water, marshes, forests, deserts, and mountaintops in all places accessible to him. If possible, he carries a pair of powerful glasses. When birds are not in sight, he "squeaks them up" by vigorously kissing the back of his hand with tight lips, thus making a mouselike squeaking sound. See

BIRD FEEDERS, BIRDHOUSES, BIRDS, CONSERVATION.

Birdhouses. Building birdhouses is one of the most gratifying of Scout projects. The Scout knows that more than fifty different kinds of North American birds have been known to nest in houses. Most of these birds are those which in a normal, wild state would have used an abandoned woodpecker's hole, or natural cavity. They include the bluebird, downy woodpecker, house wren, chickadee, crested flycatcher, flicker, screech owl, and wood duck.

The Scout learns not to make the opening in the house too large, not to place the hole near the bottom, and not to make "apartment houses" for birds other than martins. He does not use tin cans or place too many houses in a limited area. A simple

Simple birdhouses are best

house for the accommodation of the bird is much better than a fancy house made to be admired by people. See BIRD FEEDERS, BIRD HIKING, BIRDS, CONSERVATION.

Birds. A boy wanted to know if the kingfisher was a "good" or "bad" bird. He had always thought of birds in this fashion. He had been taught that a Cooper's hawk was "bad" because it fed on songbirds.

The Scout knows that in a native, wild state there are no such things as "good" or "bad" birds. All exist in a careful "balance of nature" which has developed over thousands of years. The Cooper's hawk that eats a robin is following its natural instincts in much the same way as the robin that eats a caterpillar. Each one is a check on the next. No one bird or mammal gets far out of hand, and a healthy balance results.

The individual Scout does all he can to protect birds. He works with the National Audubon Society, and he studies birds of the desert, the forest, the grasslands, and marshes. See BALANCE OF NATURE, BIRD FEEDERS, BIRD HIKING, CONSERVATION, HORNADAY AWARD, MERIT BADGES.

Biscuits. On a hike or in camp the Boy Scout bakes his own bread. These breads are known as Trail Breads, of which biscuits are the favorite.

Sometimes the Scout carries in a muslin bag a prepared biscuit flour or a mixture of 1 cup white flour, ¼ teaspoon salt, and 1½ level teaspoons baking powder, into which has been cut 2 tablespoons of shortening or lard. In camp he makes a hollow in the flour right in the bag and pours in ¼ cup of water. The mixture is stirred until the flour has soaked up all the water it will absorb. This lump of dough is placed in a pan, or wrapped around a stick, and baked.

"Sour dough" (Rancher's Bread) requires more preparation. In a bucket a medium-thick batter of 2 cups of flour and water is mixed and left until it is fermented and sour. One-half cup of the sour dough is poured out and saved for future biscuits. To the remainder are added ½ teaspoon soda, ½ teaspoon salt, 1 teaspoon melted lard, and enough flour to make a very soft dough.

Loaves are patted and put near the fire until they double in size, then baked. See BREAD ON A STICK, COOKING WITHOUT UTENSILS.

Bivouac. When night comes and an Explorer finds himself off the trail, he makes a bivouac. A bivouac is actually a temporary encampment at night without shelter, but the wise Explorer, if the weather is too wet or cold for him to sleep in the open, makes a backwoods shelter. See EXPLORER, SHELTERS.

Blinker Trainer. See SIGNALS.

Blue and Gold Dinner. A dinner for parents and friends which the Cub Scouts hold once a year, usually in connection with Boy Scout Week. Blue and gold are the Cub Scout colors. Often the mothers cook the dinner and the Cub Scouts serve it. Cub Scouts make favors and decorations for the dining table and put on a program of songs, stunts, and games. See CUB SCOUT.

Board of Review. Appearing before the Board of Review is one of the steps in advancing from Scout rank to rank. When a Scout has proved to his Troop leaders that his Scout Spirit, Scout Participation, and Scoutcraft are satisfactory, the Scoutmaster signs his certificate and the Scout reports to his Board of Review. This Board is composed of men who are friendly and sympathetic. They are usually connected with the Scout's own Troop.

They do not re-examine the Scout but question him on what he has accomplished. They want to know about his service in the Troop and to the community. They wish to be sure the Scout really practices the principles of Scouting and lives up to the Scout Oath and Law each day.

If the members of the Board of Review

feel the Scout's record is satisfactory, they approve his application for higher rank and send it to the Local Scout Council. The Scout receives his badge of rank at a Court of Honor. See ADVANCEMENT, COURT OF HONOR, SCOUT OATH AND LAW.

Boats (Building). The construction of boats and the proper handling of them are an important part of the program of Sea Exploring. Most boats are built of wood. All have a basic framework—a keel, stem, and sternpost. The ribs are attached to the keel and are held securely in place at the bottom by the keelson, which is laid on the keel. Along the upper end of the ribs, holding them in place there, is the gunwale. Over the ribs is the planking or skin. Flat-bottomed boats are built more simply. See CANOES, SAIL, SEA EXPLORER, SHIPS.

Boats (Types). Small open vessels, propelled by oars or sails. Sea Explorers speak of craft such as rowboats and lifeboats as

Small boats are handy for light sailing

"boats." However, there are thousands of types of boats, as each locality has devel-

oped its own model to suit the water conditions and the purposes for which it is used. Small yachts are called boats, but ships and steamers and larger seagoing craft are not so termed. See BOATS (BUILDING), CANOES, SAIL, SEA EXPLORER, SHIPS.

Boatswain (Bo's'n). Senior Crew Leader in Sea Exploring. The Boatswain is an elected officer. See SEA EXPLORER.

Boatswain's Pipe. A peculiar whistle, usually of silver, for summoning Sea Explorers to duty, or for directing their attention by its varied sounds. In the old days it was known as a "call."

Four positions for "calls"

Because of its antiquity and the long tradition of the boatswain's pipe as a mark of leadership, Sea Explorers have adopted it as the distinguishing mark of the Crew Leader. By holding it in four different positions in the hand while blowing it, the pipe can be made to give out a variety of tunes, or calls. See CREW LEADER, SEA EXPLORER.

Bobcat. First rank in Cub Scouting, held by an eight-year-old boy, or a newcomer to the Cub Scout program. See CUB SCOUT.

Bones, Splints, and Gauze Carnival.
Scout lingo for a First Aid Contest, in which wounds and injuries are made to appear real and demonstrations are given of their proper treatment. See FIRST AID.

Books. "Tell me what a boy reads, and I can tell you what he will probably become," said James E. West, the late Chief Scout. Scouts know how to use their school and public libraries. They learn to use the catalogues of books to choose interesting stories and books about their hobbies. Every Scout should have a library card. Many Troops have their own libraries of books on Scout subjects and Merit Badge pamphlets. Every Scout is urged to set up a bookshelf of his own, even if he has only one book to put on it. He then has the beginnings of a personal library. The Boy Scouts of America publish a free book list of books for boys. They publish also about 350 manuals and pamphlets on all Scouting subjects in addition to the *Handbook for Boys.* See BOYS' LIFE MAGAZINE, HANDBOOK FOR BOYS.

Boone, Daniel (1735-1820). American pioneer, Indian fighter, and hunter. Daniel Boone was born in Pennsylvania and was one of the first white settlers of what is today Kentucky. He was one of the men who early perfected scouting in America. His wilderness skill and ability to overcome great odds with the simple tools of the frontiersman are an inspiration to the Scout of today.

Boyce, William D. (1858-1929). The man who brought Scouting to America. He dramatically learned about the Boy Scouts during a visit to London in 1909. He had lost his way in a London fog, and a boy in uniform approached and asked if he could be of service. Having escorted Boyce to the address, the youth refused a shilling and explained, "I am a Boy Scout, and Scouts do not take tips for courtesies or Good Turns."

Boyce was so impressed that, after talking to Baden-Powell, he brought the idea of Scouting back to America. The Unknown Scout who had directed him is memorialized by a bronze statue of a buffalo in Gilwell Park, England, presented by the Boy Scouts of America, with an inscription that reads: "To the Unknown Scout whose faithfulness in the performance of the Daily Good Turn brought the Scout Movement to the United States of America." See BADEN-POWELL, BOY SCOUTS OF AMERICA.

Boy Scout. A registered member of the Boy Scouts of America from eleven through thirteen years of age. A Scout enjoys a hike through the woods with the other Scouts in his Patrol and Troop. He can tie a knot that will hold, he can climb a tree that seems impossible to others, he can swim a river, he can pitch a tent. He can find his way through the wilderness by his compass or by the stars at night. He can tell which wild plants are poisonous and which are good to eat. He can row a boat or paddle a canoe. He knows the wild animals of the forest, the birds, and the fish, and the habits and food of each.

A Scout walks through the woods with silent tread. No dry twigs snap under his feet, and no loose stones throw him off his balance. His eyes are keen, and he sees many things other boys do not notice. He reads tracks and signs on the ground and knows the creatures that made them.

A Scout can make a fire in the open on the wettest day, and he knows the secret of the Indians and can start a blaze without matches. What a meal he can prepare with his friends in the open, using few cooking pans or none at all!

The Boy Scout leads the way

His Scout Honor is his dearest possession, and he lives by his Scout Oath and Law. People turn to a Scout in time of accident or trouble, for they know he is prepared. He loves his country and his Flag and knows how to respect it. He has learned about his community and helps to serve it. He is reverent toward God, and keeps himself physically strong, mentally awake, and morally straight.

Of course, no Scout knows all these things at once. He learns more every day and finds fun and adventure all the time. First of all he is a Tenderfoot. He has learned to do some Scouting and he joins a Patrol and Troop near his home. He has a membership card and may wear the Scout uniform and his badges. There are not more than eight Scouts in a Patrol and the Patrol Leader is an older Scout. The Troop has two to four Patrols with a Senior Patrol Leader (another older Scout) and a man leader called a Scoutmaster, with Assistant Scoutmasters. The Troop has a Troop Committee and is organized by the people in a church, a men's club, a school, or other community group.

The Scout goes hiking with others in his Patrol and Troop and learns more about the out-of-doors, how to be more helpful to people, and how to take care of himself. He becomes a Scout Hiker or Second Class Scout. More service to others, a stronger Scout character, more fun in the outdoors, more skills and knowledge, and at last he is a Scout Camper—a First Class Scout.

He has learned about the Merit Badge Plan and the hobbies, interests, and projects he can have from about one hundred subjects. He works on some of them and becomes more skilled and is a better citizen. He advances in Scout rank to Star, Life, then Eagle, the highest rank of all. Before his parents and friends he proudly receives his Eagle Badge in a Court of Honor.

Scouts stand out among other boys. They are leaders. They learn to be good citizens, well trained and respected by those who know them.

Cub Scouts are eight to ten years old; Boy Scouts eleven to thirteen; Explorers fourteen years and older. Any boy can join the Scouts. The organization is open to all boys of every race. Farm boys are especially welcome. They make fine Scouts and have exciting adventures through the Scout program.

One in every two boys joins the Scout Movement sometime during his Scouting age. A boy who wants to be a Scout should ask how from another Scout or the Leader of his neighborhood Scout Unit, or he can write the National Office of the Boy Scouts of America, 2 Park Avenue, New York 16, New York. See CITIZENSHIP, CUB SCOUT, EXPLORER, PATROL, SCOUTCRAFT, SCOUT OATH AND LAW, SCOUT PARTICIPATION, SCOUT SPIRIT, TROOP.

Boy Scouts of America. A national organization chartered by Congress to teach boys how to do things for themselves and other people, to train them in Scoutcraft and teach them patriotism, courage, and self-reliance, to help them to be physically fit and to develop the kind of strong character they admire, and to learn to be good citizens.

Boys of every religious faith can join. The organization has no military or political connection.

The Boy Scouts of America was incorporated (started) on February 8, 1910, a day Boy Scouts throughout the country celebrate each year as Boy Scout Anniversary Day during Boy Scout Week.

The first Honorary President was President Taft, and since then every president of the United States has been Honorary President of the Boy Scouts. Other famous people who were first officers were Theodore Roosevelt, Honorary Vice-President and Chief Scout Citizen; Ernest Thompson Seton and Daniel Beard, authors and boy leaders; and James E. West, Chief Scout Executive.

The first edition of the *Handbook for Boys* was published in 1910, and boys everywhere rushed to join Scout Troops. Next year, 1911, the first National Office opened and the Scout Oath and Law and the first requirements of rank were adopted. These requirements were almost the same that Scouts learn today. The first Eagle Badges were earned and the first Scout Award for Heroism was made by the National Court of Honor. These were silver and bronze medals. The Gold Honor Medal was not awarded until seven years later.

Sea Scouting started in 1912, the only program for older Scouts. *Boys' Life* magazine was purchased to give news about Scouts and stories and articles on Scouting. Next year the first Hornaday Conservation Awards for Wildlife Protection were made. The first national Bird Feeding Good Turn took place in the winter, and Scouts of New York State set out thousands of trees in the first national Scout Tree Planting project. All the time Scouting was growing, more and more boys were coming in, people understood better what

Scouts help in flood rescue work

Scouting stands for, and Scouts did Good Turns in their community. They helped in floods, in fires, and in other emergencies.

On June 15, 1916, because of the help that Scouts had given, Congress granted a Federal charter to the Boy Scouts of America. This charter protects the badges and uniforms of Scouting so that no one who is not a Scout may wear them.

The badges the early Scouts wore were about the same as today. The uniform included khaki breeches and puttees, a long coat with big pockets, and a high hat with a broad floppy brim—quite unlike the smart uniform Scouts now wear!

In World War I, Scouts were put to a real test. They did themselves proud. They sold Liberty Bonds, distributed literature for the government, and did many other services. In 1920 the first World Jamboree was held in England, with Scouts from thirty-two countries living and camping together. Since then World Jamborees have been held every four years except during the war, with many thousands of Scouts from all over the world taking part. International Conferences of Scout Leaders started the same year and are held every two years.

Boy Scouts hold National Jamborees in the United States. The first was in Washington in 1937 and the second at Valley Forge, Pennsylvania, in 1950. Forty-seven thousand Scouts and Leaders attended. National Jamborees are scheduled for every four years.

Cub Scouting (for younger boys) started in 1930. The old Explorer program started in 1933 and Air Scouting in 1941. In 1949 the three Senior Scout branches were combined in the new Explorer program. That same year the ages for each of the programs of Scouting were lowered by one one year.

During World War II every Scout did his best to help win the war. The government made sixty-nine requests for Boy Scout war service. Outstanding among these were campaigns to collect waste paper, which General Eisenhower recognized with an

A waste-paper collection drive

award. There were collections of metal salvage, clothing, and of many other needed items. Scouts distributed millions of circulars, posters, and other government publications. Twenty thousand Scouts earned the General Douglas MacArthur Medal for growing food. Scouts developed the World Friendship Fund to help rebuild Scouting abroad at the end of the war. They sent money, Scout equipment, Scout uniforms, books, and badges to their Scout brothers.

There are two magnificent National Scout Reservations. One of these, the Schiff Scout Reservation, is located in Mendham, New Jersey, and is a memorial to the man who helped found Scouting and was president of the organization at the time of his death. His mother presented this reservation in his memory. The National Training Center for Professional Scout Leaders is located at Schiff.

The other is Philmont Scout Ranch at Cimarron, New Mexico, consisting of 127,-000 acres, given by Waite Phillips. It offers wilderness camping to Explorers and includes a Training Center for volunteer Scout leaders.

In 1952 the Boy Scouts of America inaugurated a Three Year Program with the slogan "Forward on Liberty's Team." Every Scout and Leader was given the opportunity to take part in making this Three Year Program a success. It was the avowed purpose to make the boys, the Scout Movement, and the nation physically strong, mentally awake, and morally straight.

At the end of 1911, the first full year of Scouting, there were 61,495 Scouts and Scouters throughout the United States. During 1952 the active membership reached 3,000,000. Over 19,000,000 persons have belonged to Scouting since it was first founded. See BADEN-POWELL, BEARD, BOYCE, BOY SCOUT WEEK, CONSERVATION, HANDBOOK FOR BOYS, JAMBOREE (NATIONAL), JAMBOREE (WORLD), UNIFORMS.

Boy Scout Statuette. The official statuette designed by Dr. R. Tait McKenzie, famous sculptor and pioneer member of the Philadelphia Scout Council. It is of a Boy Scout with uncovered head, symbolizing

The Boy Scout Statuette

reverence and obedience to proper authorities. Thousands of these official statuettes have been used by Troops and individuals as gifts. The original life-size statue stands in front of the Scout office in Philadelphia.

Boy Scout Week. Observed in February each year by all Scouts, in honor of the founding of the organization. Boy Scout Week includes always February 8, Scout Anniversary Day, and February 12, Lincoln's Birthday.

Boys' Life Magazine. Official magazine for all Scouts, published monthly by the Boy Scouts of America. It was started in 1912 as a part of the reading program of Boy Scouts. It seeks to publish the kind of stories boys like—adventure, humor, sports, and science fiction. It includes articles on Scouting activities, camping and outdoor features, fishing tricks, fly-making, mountain climbing, skiing, snowshoeing, horsemanship, canoeing, boating, tent making, pack making, log cabins, temporary shelters, igloos, cave exploration, cruises, mapping, handicrafts, hunting, first aid, and survival.

Brave, A Scout Is. The tenth part of the Scout Law. It says:

"A SCOUT IS BRAVE. He has courage to face danger in spite of fear, and to stand up for the right against the coaxing of friends or the jeers or threats of enemies, and defeat does not down him." See SCOUT OATH AND LAW.

Bread on a Stick. One of the Trail Breads, baked over an open fire. In making this bread the Scout may use one of the prepared biscuit flours (1 cup of prepared flour to a person), mixing it with milk or water. The dough is made a little firmer than for ordinary biscuits. Sometimes it is worked into a ribbon and twisted around a stick of sweet-tasting wood. Another way is to stir the dough with a stick until the dough hangs onto the stick. The stick is then placed in front of the fire or over the coals and the dough carefully baked on all sides by turning the stick. See BISCUITS.

Breeches Buoy. A life saving or rescue device, sometimes termed a "life car,"

Breeches buoy ready for rescue work

consisting of canvas breeches attachable at the waist to a ring-shaped life buoy, which are slung and run upon a rope stretched from the shore to a vessel in distress. A shot with a long line attached is fired across the endangered ship to establish contact. Sometimes breeches buoys are used from one ship to another. Sea Explorers are schooled in making and using this important rescue apparatus. See SEA EXPLORER.

Bridge of Honor. A Court of Honor ceremony held by Sea Explorers when Advancement Awards are made. The Bridge of Honor is a gala affair to which girl friends and parents are invited. Tradition has made it a formal affair. See SEA EXPLORER.

Bridger, James (1804-81). Famous scout and explorer, sometimes called "the Daniel Boone of the Rockies." Born in Richmond, Virginia, Bridger went west at an early age. By the time he was sixteen he already had won a reputation as a scout. He explored nearly the whole region included in the present states of Montana, Idaho, Wyoming, Utah, and the Dakotas. He discovered the wonders of Yellowstone Park and the Great Salt Lake. With a piece of charcoal and a buffalo hide he could map an entire area. Other scouts claimed Jim Bridger "could smell his way if he did not see it." Named for him are Bridger's Pass in Wyoming, Bridger's Peak in Montana, and the towns of Bridger and Fort Bridger in Wyoming. See EXPLORER.

Bridges. Some Scouts stand on the bank of a stream. It is here they will erect a bridge. They have selected the site carefully. The stream is straight at this point and the ground is firm and the bank will not wash away.

"The water is sort of swift. I think a Straddle Bug would be the thing," says one Scout.

"Why don't we make a Stringer while we are about it?" suggests another.

"You forget we don't have any spikes. Almost have to have spikes for a Stringer."

"Yeah, that's right. I think a Monkey Bridge will do here. Then we won't need anything but our axes—no nails, wire, or spikes. We have all the rope we need in camp."

"That's it! A Monkey Bridge it will be!"

They start to work on a Monkey Bridge, one of the most primitive types of bridges, one that swings and sways plenty but which will span the stream.

The *Monkey Bridge* has two shear legs with the cross about four feet from the upper tips. A shear is anchored on each side of the stream. The foot rope is about an inch in diameter and passes directly over the cross of the shear legs, resting on some bagging or moss to keep it from chafing. It is also anchored at each end by a series of "hold-fasts." The hand ropes are tied to the upper tips of the shear legs and laced to the foot rope. Although this bridge is simple, care must be used in making it so that the balance is not destroyed.

The *Light Pole Bridge* is similar to the Monkey Bridge, except that poles are used instead of ropes. It is a good shallow-water bridge. The *Straddle Bug* is a basic form of bridge—a series of "horses" connected by a walking platform. It is especially good for swift water as the "bug" legs soon become buried firmly in the bottom of the stream.

Stringer bridges are a more permanent form of bridge and can be built to support a team and wagon or an automobile. *Lock* bridges are built on the basic Stringer idea but cover a greater span by use of supporting diagonals.

Scouts can build bridges that will carry heavy loads

Bridges are important, and Scouts and Explorers know how to build—without nails, spikes, or wire—a bridge or derrick capable of supporting two hundred pounds in weight, as a part of the Merit Badge requirements for Pioneering. See EXPLORER, FIRST CLASS SCOUT, HOLDFAST, LASHINGS, MERIT BADGES, PIONEERING.

Buddy Plan. One of the important water-safety rules at Scout camps. Scouts are paired off as buddies and swim together at all times. The safety rule states: "Always swim with a buddy and keep within ten feet of him all the time." See SWIMMING.

Budget Plan. A businesslike system of finance for all Scouting Units. The budget is carefully planned by the Scouts themselves.

Each Scout pays a certain small amount in weekly dues, which he usually earns himself, to cover such things as registration, badges, subscription to *Boys' Life* magazine, *Good Turn*, and other items. The Treasurer collects the dues, deposits them, and keeps a record of expenses. This puts the Unit on a pay-as-you-go basis. See THRIFTY, A SCOUT IS.

Bugling. "You can't get 'em up, you can't get 'em up, you can't get 'em up in the morning!" So goes Reveille. Most Scout camps use bugle calls to announce activities to Scouts. There is Reveille to get them up in the morning, Mess Call for food, Swimming Call, To the Colors and Retreat for raising and lowering the United States Flag, and other calls with specific meanings. Bugling is a Merit Badge subject, and many Scouts practice until they become exceptional buglers. Some Troops use bugle calls for a Troop camp and Troop activities, if they have a good bugler. See MERIT BADGES.

The bugle calls Scouts together

Burnham, Major Frederick Russell (1861-1947). American soldier and explorer. He also was noted as an Indian fighter, hunter, cattle rancher, scout, and guide in Arizona, Africa, and Alaska's Klondike. He was scout and guide through two Matabele wars in Africa and chief scout of the British Army during the Boer War. He was a friend of Baden-Powell and taught him many of the skills of Scouting. He kept perfectly fit, and at eighty he was so quick that he could snatch a fly out of the air with his fingers! He wrote *Scouting on Two Continents*.

Burro. A donkey popular in the mountain sections of the West as a pack animal. This patient little animal is used by Explorers at Philmont Scout Ranch to carry their duffel and equipment on the difficult mountain trails. See PHILMONT SCOUT RANCH.

Byrd, Admiral Richard E. (1888—) American naval commander, aviator, and polar explorer. In 1926 Admiral Byrd made the first airplane flight over the North Pole. In 1927-28 he organized the Antarctic Exploring Expedition and in 1929 made the first flight over the South Pole. Byrd took a Scout with him to the South Pole, Paul A. Siple. See SIPLE.

Caches. Places for concealing or storing food. The Scout sometimes finds it necessary to cache food on ropes or sticks suspended between trees to keep it safe from animals, or to store it in some safe place

A simple tree cache

for future use. Sometimes an underground cache is the most practical, the Scout being careful to replace the sod or leaves over the filled hole in which his food is stored. Of course, this can only be done with food that is not perishable. See CAMPING (ADVENTURE), EXPLORER.

Campfire Ceremonies. As if by magic the flames of the roaring campfire conjure from the darkness of night a large and comfortable room. The tall, overhanging trees are highlighted into walls and ceiling. Around the fire is a circle of bright, eager faces. The Scoutmaster announces:

"As the flames point upward so be our aim. As the red logs glow so be our sympathies. As the gray ash fades so be our errors. As the good fire warms the circle so may our ideals warm the world. I now declare the council open."

This is the time for relaxation, fun, and song. Sometimes the Scouts put on a dramatic sketch or a funny stunt. Or the Scoutmaster may tell campfire stories. Often they give Indian dances in beautiful costumes, or perform a solemn Indian ceremony. One group or another may have charge of the program on different nights. See CAMPING (LONG-TERM).

Camping (Adventure). A rugged or venturesome type of camping. The Scout of advanced rank, or the Explorer, puts into practice all his knowledge of Scoutcraft, wood lore, and wildlife. This kind of camping may come as a part of extended hikes off the beaten paths of civilization: bicycle trips, canoe trips, and skiing trips.

Adventure Camping is realized to its

The start of an adventurous packsaddle trip

fullest in packsaddle trips into the mountains at Philmont Scout Ranch and canoe trips from established canoe bases in Wisconsin and Minnesota.

The Scout gives considerable thought to this camping trip. He wants to make it comfortable and enjoyable. It is not the Scout's idea to make himself needlessly uncomfortable. He does not associate camping with sleeping on the cold, hard ground without adequate blankets or a sleeping bag or shelter, remaining awake half the night with cold feet, or with rain seeping down his neck and back. He does not relish burned biscuits or heavy, soggy griddle cakes. He does not consider it a necessary evil to return with several bad blisters, infection from poison ivy, or his body covered with mosquito bites.

The Scout has planned the proper clothing for the weather and the place. He has packed neither too much nor too little duffel. He travels light and far and he has a good time. When his camping trip is over, he is richer in a satisfying experience.

Camping is much more than just fun and frolic outdoors. The Scout knows that in becoming an expert camper he is acquiring a skill that may be vitally important to him someday. It may help him in his life's work as an engineer who builds bridges across jungle rivers and ravines, or across high mountain canyons. Or as a surveyor who lays out transcontinental highways. Or possibly as an aviation expert who constructs landing fields in a wilderness area. It may prove important to him as a mining engineer or in many other professions which demand a knowledge of camping and outdoor living.

Then there is the thrill experienced by the Scout, especially if he has lived in a city, who has such confidence in himself, because of the skills he has learned, that he and his Patrol can plunge into the forest or mountains and live like pioneers. He knows that he can make fire by friction, that he can sleep comfortably under a shelter that he himself has erected with only his axe, that his keen eye can spot plants that are good for eating and enable him to avoid those that are injurious, that he can fashion a fishing line from twisted bark.

But the most satisfying feeling is that he is at home with Nature. He knows the trees and the birds and the mammals. He can tell the stars by name and find his way by them. He can read the weather in the formations of clouds. He knows what to do in all kinds of emergencies. He is prepared.

This kind of living was once the natural state of man, and the Scout feels that when he learns it he has come into his own. He has realized the heritage of the pioneers. See BOY SCOUT, CANOE BASE, EXPLORER, HIKES (KINDS OF), PHILMONT SCOUT RANCH.

Camping (Long-Term). Camping for a week or more in one place. This is the biggest event of the Scouting year, and to the average Scout the long-term summer camp is the greatest adventure in Scouting. The Scout plans for it during the winter, makes his own equipment, and practices his skills on short-term or week-end camps. The members of the Troop Leaders Council hold many meetings and plan for equipment, grub, program, and other things. Every detail is carefully worked out beforehand and duties assigned to responsible leaders.

During the summer camp the Scout each day finds his muscles becoming harder, his skin taking on more sun tan, the fresh air invigorating him more and more. All the time he is having fun, yet at the same time he is also learning many valuable lessons.

Summer camping brings fun and adventure

He is developing some of the resourcefulness and self-reliance of the pioneer. He is advancing in Scouting. He is learning teamwork and team play, how to get along with other boys, and how to do his share in common, everyday duties. He is advancing in rank as he acquires new skills.

The ideal way for Long-Term Camping is when the Troop camps under its own leadership with its own Scoutmaster, Assistants, and Patrol Leaders.

The Troop may camp at the Council campsite or may go to some other campsite. The Troop then provides its own camping gear, from tentage to waterfront equipment, and develops its own sanitary arrangements. It depends on its own leadership to live up to Council regulations and National Camping Standards. This is known as Troop Camping.

In the Council camp the tents, cooking gear, and other equipment may be furnished by the camp. The Council makes sanitary arrangements, tests the water supply, and provides medical attention. Trained leaders are in charge of swimming and boating and health supervision. Experts are available to help with Scoutcraft, nature lore, and other activities.

There are some Patrols that, in addition to taking part in the Troop camp, like to extend summer camping by a long-term camp of their own for a week or more. Each day adds up to the fifty days required for the Merit Badge in camping. See Camping (Adventure), Camporee, Merit Badges, "Overnight," Patrol Camping, Troop Camping, Winter Camping.

Camp Log. A record of the daily events of camp, kept by the Troop or Patrol Scribe. Some camp logs are elaborate, bound in birchbark or buckskin or polished wood, and illustrated with photographs and souvenirs of the camp. See Camping (Long-Term).

Camporee. A demonstration of camping skills by Troops and Patrols which set up their own camps for one or more days and nights. At a Camporee there is fun and good-fellowship and a mutual opportunity to learn more about camping.

Many Local Councils hold Camporees each year, usually in the spring. Troops and Patrols do not compete against one another but against a standard, so that all have an opportunity to win recognition. Observers, who keep score, first inspect each Patrol. They check the Scouts' packs to see if they are properly packed. They check to see if Patrol equipment is properly distributed and if personal equipment is sufficient. They particularly observe the appearance of each Scout.

Then the real excitement begins. The Tenting Crews put up tents and make beds, and the Cooking Crews build fireplaces, get wood and water, set out pots and pans, and cook the grub.

The observers check all these activities and make notes on general appearance. They check to see whether the tents are properly located, trenched in case of rain,

and with well-constructed, comfortable beds. They see if every Scout has a definite duty and if he performs it satisfactorily. Then the scores are added up.

Scouts show camping skills at Camporees

Troops also hold their own Camporees to get ready for the District or Council Camporee. These may occur any time during the year and are on a Patrol basis. See Camping (Long-Term), Patrol Camping, Troop Camping.

Canada, Scouting in. In 1908, when the publication of *Scouting for Boys* in Great Britain brought Scouting into being, groups of boys all over Canada banded themselves together into Troops and called themselves Boy Scouts.

The pattern of the Scout program in Canada follows closely that in use throughout the British Commonwealth. The Movement is divided into three sections: Wolf Cubs, Boy Scouts, and Rover Scouts. Sea Scouts are part of the Boy Scout Branch, and Rover Sea Scouts of the Rover Scout Branch. Wolf Cubs range in age from eight to twelve, Boy Scouts from twelve to eighteen, and Rover Scouts from sixteen to twenty-three.

31

The Wolf Cub program is based on the *Jungle Books* by Rudyard Kipling and is quite different from the Cub Scout program in the United States. The ranks in Cubbing are Tenderpad, First Star, and

Boy Scouts of Canada

Second Star. The Cub uniform consists of a green cap with gold piping, a green sweater, blue shorts, blue stockings with green tops, and the Pack neckerchief.

The Boy Scout program, while differing in requirements of rank, is similar to that of the United States, except that a top ranking Scout in Canada is called a King's Scout (possibly to be changed to Queen's Scout), whereas in the United States he is an Eagle Scout. The Canadian rank originated in an interview which the founder of Scouting, Lord Baden-Powell, had with King Edward VII, who suggested that Scouts specially trained for community service be called "King's Scouts." Thus all qualifying badges for a King's Scout are designed to make a boy efficient in the service of his home and community. Among these badges are Ambulance Man, Path-

finder, Fireman, Cyclist, Rescuer, and Public-Health Man.

Rover Scouts were called by Baden-Powell, "The Brotherhood of the Open Air." Their principal activities are hiking, exploring, and preparation for manhood by study of the customs and heritage of the country and learning about various vocations by which they may earn their living.

At the end of 1951 there were 128,000 Wolf Cubs, Boy Scouts, Rover Scouts, and Scouters in Canada. These figures do not include the thousands of members of Group Committees, Ladies Auxiliaries, and Council members.

Canadian Boy Scouts Association.
Scouting in Canada operates under a Royal Charter granted by King Edward VII and for many years was a branch of the British Boy Scouts Association. However, in 1914 the Canadian General Council of the Boy Scouts Association was incorporated by Act of Parliament, and the Governor-General at that time, the Duke of Connaught, became the first Chief Scout for Canada. Since that time the office of Chief Scout has been held traditionally by the Governor-General.

Canadian Headquarters of the Boy Scout Association is located at 306 Metcalfe Street, in Ottawa, the nation's capital.

Under the Act of Parliament the Canadian General Council is empowered to form other councils and delegate powers to these councils. Thus, in each of the ten provinces, Provincial Councils have been formed, each with its own headquarters and headed by a Provincial President, Provincial Commissioner, and a Provincial Executive Commissioner who supervises the administrative and field staff operations.

Provincial Councils, in turn, delegate powers to District Councils, which in larger centers have their own headquarters and

Cub Scouts play home made games together

executive staff. In Canada, at the end of 1951, the field staff totaled sixty-five Executive and Field Commissioners, in addition to a large number of secretarial employees.

A national supply service, or Stores Department as it is known in Canada, is conducted by Canadian Headquarters for the supply of uniforms, badges, books, and equipment.

Candidate Scout. A registered Scout who is not yet a Tenderfoot. To become a Candidate Scout a boy must be at least eleven years old. He must be able to repeat from memory the Scout Oath or Promise, the twelve points of the Scout Law, the Scout Motto, and the Scout Slogan and explain the meaning of each in his own words. A Candidate Scout does not have a rank, but he is a registered member of a Troop and Patrol and has the right to wear the uniform. His first rank is that of Tenderfoot. See BOY SCOUT, TENDERFOOT SCOUT.

Canoe Bases. Outfitting bases for canoe trips into the North Country. There are two of these bases established and maintained by the Boy Scouts of America to give Explorers an opportunity for wilderness canoe trips filled with high adventure.

The Region VII Explorer Canoe Base is located on White Sand Lake, near Boulder Junction, Wisconsin. Region X Sommers Wilderness Canoe Base is on Moose Lake, near Ely, Minnesota.

All Explorers in Troops, Posts, Squadrons, or Ships may take these trips, which take place during the summer. Explorers must be able to swim and should have had some camping experience.

In Region VII, when a group of Explorers plans to take a trip from one of the canoe bases with the approval of their Council, they first select one of their members who

is seventeen years of age or older. This Explorer is sent ahead to one of the base camps for six days of intensive wilderness canoe training. No charge is made for this training. On completing the course he becomes the *voyageur,* or guide, for the party. Each group also must have an adult leader over twenty-one.

Region X sends an experienced adult guide with each Crew, in addition to the Crew's own adult leader.

Before leaving home Explorers are urged to make a few practice trips to get in some camping, cooking, canoeing, and swimming and check their party organization. They also study the pamphlet, *A Guide Book for Canoe Trails,* published jointly by Regions VII and X.

The trips are for ten-day periods. On arrival at the base camp Explorers find a

Carrying a canoe across a portage

twenty-four-hour program has been established to help in preparing them. Equipment is furnished at the base camp. Two, or not more than three, boys are assigned to each canoe.

Now begins the adventurous camping program which is the heart of Exploring. The Explorers travel by day, paddling

33

along streams or carrying their canoes over portages. They camp at night and prepare their own food. They are in a country that abounds in wildlife and fish.

The Explorer paddles along historic water trails, for canoeing in the North Country is not of modern origin. For centuries the Indians paddled the lakes and streams of Canada, Minnesota, Wisconsin, and Michigan. Then came the French *voyageurs* in the middle of the seventeenth century. With the *voyageurs* came the establishment of the fur-company outposts. After them came the lumberjacks.

Canoe trips, like the packsaddle trips in the mountains at Philmont Scout Ranch, provide adventuresome camping opportunities for Explorers. See CANOEING, EXPLORER, PHILMONT SCOUT RANCH.

Canoeing. Whether in camp or on extended trips through the wilderness canoe country, canoeing is one of the most enjoyable activities of the Scout.

Everyone likes canoeing

The Scout learns to paddle the canoe from the kneeling position. Seats in canoes raise the body of the occupant too high above the center of gravity of the craft and make the canoe unsteady and likely to upset. The Scout uses thirty-two paddle strokes to the minute and learns a variety of strokes, as well as how to steer. He practices getting out of a canoe and then back in without upsetting it. Good canoeists may try for the Canoeing Merit Badge. See CANOE BASE, CANOES, MERIT BADGES.

Canoes. Light boats propelled by paddles. The modern canoe is adapted from the Indian birch-bark canoe, one of the Indian's most important gifts to the white man and civilization. The white man's canoe is canvas covered and, like that of the Indian, is light and easily carried over portages. It draws little water and can be paddled in narrow and shallow streams.

For ordinary stream travel with portages, the Scout selects a sixteen-foot canoe weighing about sixty-five pounds. Larger rivers or lakes require a heavier type—one of eighteen feet and weighing about ninety pounds. All types have an open gunwale so they can drain easily. The keel should be long and straight and the bottom flat. See CANOE BASE, CANOEING.

Carries. Methods and devices for transporting injured persons. The proper "carry," or way of moving a patient, is of utmost importance in first aid. Excellent first aid measures may be offset by improper carrying or handling of a person suffering from a head injury, fractured skull, broken back, or leg fractures. The first rule is, "Don't move fracture cases until the doctor gets there." If this rule cannot be kept, put on splints first.

Scouts know the proper method of transporting or carrying injured persons. They learn that a severely injured person should always be carried on a stretcher, and if the best type of stretcher, the "army" stretcher, is not available, they know how to impro-

The Three-Man Carry

vise one. Sometimes it is necessary to transport the patient by other means.

In the *Three-Man Carry*, three bearers kneel on the same side of the injured person, always on the side opposite to that of any serious injury. With the arms placed under the patient's head, shoulders, back, hips, and legs he is raised to the knees of the bearers at the command to lift, and as they stand up slowly with him cradled in their arms they roll him toward them so the front of his body is against their chests.

The Packstrap Carry

Another method is known as the *Six or Eight-Bearer Carry*. While eight bearers are best, six will do if they are strong

and the patient is light. Standing three or four on either side, the bearers slide their hands and arms gently under the head, the body just past the lower end of the spine, the thighs, and legs of the injured person, and at the command "Lift!" they carefully rise, keeping the person level and lifting him on the hands and forearms. For a short distance a side step is best.

The *Pack-Strap Carry* is executed by one person. The patient's arms are brought over the bearer's shoulders from the back and crossed in front of the bearer's chest. Care is taken that the bearer's shoulders are well up in the armpits of the patient.

The woodsman's "go-devil"

There are other types of carries employed by Scouts. When in the woods, away from civilization, and it is found necessary to transport an injured person, the Scouts construct drag litters based on the American Indian travois. A similar drag, to be pulled by a man and known as the woodsman's "go-devil," is made with shorter poles and a strap which passes behind the neck and in front of the shoulders, much like those of pack straps. See FIRST AID.

Carson, Christopher (Kit), (1809–68). American hunter, trapper, and western scout. Carson was born in Madison County, Kentucky, and at the age of seventeen accompanied a party of hunters to Santa Fé, New Mexico. After this he devoted himself almost entirely to hunting and trapping, and his hairbreadth escapes and personal prowess became subjects of numerous stories. He served as a guide in Frémont's famous expeditions to California. He later served with the United States Army and in 1865 was brevetted a brigadier general.

Ceremonies. The Scout is inspired by Scout ideals and helped to realize his obligations as a Scout by dignified, simple ceremonies. There are Advancement ceremonies, recognizing Scouts who advance to higher ranks, Troop Installation ceremonies, Investiture ceremonies, and many others.

The Scoutmaster sees that ceremonies are worked out carefully and approved by the Troop Leaders' Council. Units are encouraged to develop new and interesting ceremonies of their own. See BRIDGE OF HONOR, CAMPFIRE CEREMONIES, COURT OF HONOR, INVESTITURE CEREMONIES.

Certificate of Heroism. An award for heroism in saving a life at personal risk, which is given the Scout by the National Court of Honor. See GOLD HONOR MEDAL, NATIONAL COURT OF HONOR.

Certificate of Service. An honorable discharge given a Scout who, for good reason, finds it impossible to keep up his Scouting connections, for a time at least. The certificate, issued by the Scoutmaster, indicates the rank and service record of the Scout, and cites that he is in good standing.

Chanteys. "Oh, blow the man down, laddies," lustily sing the Sea Explorer Crew.

Sea Explorers sing old-time chanteys

The uniformed group, led by the chanteyman or song leader, are entertaining at the District meeting. When they finish, there is much applause. Chanteys today remain as a part of the sea lore that makes Sea Exploring so fascinating to the Scout. They are sung at regattas, rendezvous, Camporees, and around campfires. See SEA EXPLORER.

Chaplain. A clergyman of any denomination having official charge of religious services and the spiritual welfare of Scout Units or camps. A Unit Chaplain is appointed by the sponsoring institution. In Council camps he is appointed by the Council. He is a registered member of the Boy Scouts of America and has a badge showing his leadership responsibility.

Character (Scout). Three things are important to the character of the Boy Scout. There is Scout Spirit, which the boy develops as he strives his best to learn more about and live up to the ideals and traditions of Scouting; Scout Participation, which he demonstrates as he engages in Unit activities and service projects, and helps in home, school, church, and community; and Scoutcraft, which he learns as he becomes a good outdoorsman and which helps develop self-reliant character and good citizenship. See SCOUTCRAFT, SCOUT PARTICIPATION, SCOUT SPIRIT.

Charcoal Cooking. There are times when Scouts encamp in Federal and State parks where open fires are prohibited in the dry months of summer. Cooking is then done by charcoal. The Scout is always careful to conform with local rules and strives to leave the place on which he has camped just as he found it—or cleaner. When forty thousand Scouts held their National Jamboree at Valley Forge, Pennsylvania, in the summer of 1950, they encamped on the park's lawnlike carpet of grass. Cooks of five thousand patrols prepared the meals

Outdoor cooking over a charcoal stove

over charcoal, burned in stoves, many of which were made by the Scouts themselves. Not a blade of grass was destroyed.

Charcoal is used also in back yards when barbecues are prepared for the family and fellow Scouts. See JAMBOREE (NATIONAL).

Charter. Every institution sponsoring a Scout Unit receives a charter from the National Council to organize and maintain its Unit. Every Local Council also receives a charter to promote and supervise Scouting within its area. The National Organization was granted a Federal charter by Congress. See BOY SCOUTS OF AMERICA, LOCAL COUNCIL.

Cheerful, A Scout Is. The eighth point of the Scout Law. It states: "A SCOUT IS CHEERFUL. He smiles whenever he can. His obedience to orders is prompt and cheery. He never shirks nor grumbles at hardships." See SCOUT OATH AND LAW.

Chowder. An easily prepared and tasty dish made by the Scout camper. He cleans, bones, flakes, and parboils a fish for a few minutes. Then in a pot he puts diced onions (wild onions if he has them), salt pork or camp meatfat, salt and pepper, and the water in which the fish was boiled. The pot is placed over the fire and, when the contents are stewing nicely, he adds the fish. The chowder is cooked until all is tender. Potatoes can be added.

Church. "A SCOUT IS REVERENT" is the twelfth point in the Scout Law. The Scout does his part in his church by learning the teachings and ideals of his religion, and by living up to his beliefs in his everyday life.

The Scout is regular in attendance and active in participation in religious services in his church or synagogue. He helps out whenever he can and makes himself a good example for younger members. Leadership experience in Scouting aids him in leading church clubs and other religious groups. See SCOUT OATH AND LAW.

Circus. "Right this way, ladies and gentlemen, and see the greatest side show on earth! . . . See Bertha, the Bearded Lady . . . Jo-Jo, the Dog-faced Boy . . . Sheila, the Snake Charmer! . . . Step right up . . . buy your tickets here!"

The barker, standing on a platform in front of the side-show tent, gives a twirl to his Blackie Daw mustache. He waves his gold-headed cane toward the entrance to the Greatest Side Show on Earth. A heavy gold chain sparkles across his vest.

The Circus has come to town! The Pack Circus of the local Cub Scouts. If it is a warm night, the Big Top has been erected

Cub Scouts make gay circus costumes

outside in the "circus grounds." Otherwise it is set up in the school gymnasium. Fathers and mothers and friends are out to enjoy the fun.

Posters and signs have been placed around the town announcing the coming attraction. And just as in any big circus, there has been a parade!

Usually the parents take their boys to the circus. But turnabout is fair play. Now the boys are giving a circus for their parents and friends.

The Pack Circus marks the end of a month of fun for the Cub Scouts. Each Den has had its special program, each with a circus theme, climaxed with the big

Pack Circus at the monthly Pack meeting.

Dens made all the large animals for the circus parade. They made the costumes and properties for the acts. Many of these acts already had been put on for parents at Den meetings. So there would be no duplication in acts they were reported to the Cubmaster. At the big circus they are all combined.

The Pack Circus is one of the biggest and most enjoyable events on the Cub Scout program. See CUB SCOUT.

Citizenship. A boy is walking along the street, hands in his pockets, whistling. He sees something shining in the gutter. It is a piece of broken bottle. He walks over, picks it up, and starts away. A man who is behind him calls to him.

"I saw you pick up that piece of glass, son," he said in a kindly tone. "I am curious to know why you did it."

"I was afraid it would cut someone's automobile tire if he drove over it when he parked there," promptly replied the boy.

"I see," said the man. "Does your family own a car?"

"No, sir," answered the boy. "But it would be bad for someone who did own one. That's what I was thinking about."

"My boy, you are going to be a fine citizen when you grow up. This is a very small thing, but you did it without any thought of thanks from anyone—just because you wanted to help others. Is that right?"

"Yes, sir."

"I am proud to have met you. This kind of service to the community is the first step in citizenship—this doing things for others without thought of reward. I suppose you are a Boy Scout."

"I am a Scout, sir."

The Scout and man each went his way. The Scout knew that his small service, like other types of service for others without expecting a reward, has much to do with good citizenship.

Yet the Scout knew he did get a reward when he performed a service. It was not a reward in money, or even in thanks. The reward was the good feeling he had when

A Scout learns how to be a citizen

he knew he had helped someone, or made someone happy or more contented with life. Even small services are fine things, and he knew that people who do fine things feel fine after doing them.

Citizenship training is a goal in Scouting. The trail to citizenship carries through Cub Scouting, Boy Scouting, and Exploring. The good Scout most likely becomes the good citizen.

Citizenship involves working for the community in which you live. There have been many ways of expressing this idea in days gone by. People through the ages had their codes of good citizenship. There was the Law of Moses. The Athenian Oath. Knights of the Round Table pledged their honor to uphold the right. There was the Mayflower Compact. Our Declaration of Independence.

The pioneers of this country, when banded together into a community, observed the rule, "All for one and one for all." They held husking bees and barn

raisings where everyone pitched in to help his neighbor.

There were reasons for these codes, compacts, and declarations. They helped the individual to grow into a better man and a better citizen.

Three requirements—character, participation, and leadership—are the basis of good citizenship as well as good Scouting and Exploring. The Scout does not need to wait until he is twenty-one to practice citizenship. All around him are chances to become a good citizen. Citizenship is more than voting and holding public office. It is doing his share wherever he is. It is his Scout Spirit of helpfulness, plus the knowledge and skills that he carries with him every day. See ATHENIAN OATH, CHARACTER (SCOUT), CITIZENSHIP DEDICATION, SCOUT CODE, SCOUT PARTICIPATION.

A part of our national heritage

Citizenship Dedication. Exploring is the trail to citizenship. In whatever way it leads the young man to serve his community, it makes him more able to have or enjoy citizenship in common with others and makes him better trained for a voting citizenship when he becomes of age.

The Explorer citizen dedicates himself to the following:

1. I will live the Scout Oath and Law.
2. I will be familiar with the Declaration

39

of Independence, the Constitution of the United States, and the Bill of Rights.

3. I will respect and obey the law in order to have security and freedom.

4. I will share the responsibility of my home, school, church, neighborhood, and community; and when legally of age, I will register and vote in all elections.

5. I will deal fairly and kindly with my fellow-citizens of whatever race or creed, in the spirit of the Scout Law and America's tradition of equality of opportunity.

6. I will work to preserve our American heritage of liberty and responsibility. I acknowledge that the privileges we enjoy were won by the hard work and sacrifices, faith and clear thinking, of our forefathers. I will do all in my power to pass on a better America to the next generation. See CITIZENSHIP, EXPLORER, SCOUT OATH AND LAW.

Clean, A Scout Is. The eleventh point of the Scout Law. It states: "A SCOUT IS CLEAN. He keeps clean in body and thought, stands for clean speech, clean sport, clean habits, and travels with a clean crowd." See SCOUT OATH AND LAW.

Clock Time. Time measured and indicated by clocks and watches. There are two systems of clock time in Scouting. One is the twelve-hour clock time and the other the twenty-four-hour clock time. The latter is used by Sea Explorers and Air Explorers. As in the United States Army, Air Corps, and Navy, time is marked by the twenty-four-hour system, where the day begins at midnight. Example: 8 A.M. is designated 0800 and spoken of as "0 eight hundred hours." Sea Explorers use "bell time." See BELL TIME, SEA EXPLORER.

Clouds. Masses of visible vapor floating in the air. Clouds are valuable in predicting weather. There are ten cloud families, and after learning to identify each, the Scout learns to "read" it and tell what it signifies.

What are termed "high clouds," with an average lower level of 20,000 feet, include *cirrus,* or thin, featherlike clouds; *cirro-cumulus,* thin clouds, cotton or flakelike; and *cirrostratus,* very thin sheet clouds. "Middle clouds," averaging between 6,500 feet and 20,000 feet, are *altocumulus,* sheep-backlike clouds, and *altostratus,* medium high uniform sheet clouds. "Low clouds," below 6,500 feet, are *stratocumulus,* globular masses; *stratus,* low uniform sheet clouds; *nimbostratus,* low, shapeless, and rainy-layer clouds; and *scud,* loose, vapory clouds. Vertical clouds, from 1,600 feet to more than 20,000 feet, are *cumulus,* dense, dome-shaped and puffy looking; and *cumulonimbus,* towering clouds.

The Scout knows that when some clouds follow each other in procession a storm is brewing. Light, delicate clouds in soft, fluffy masses foretell fair weather. In general, the Scout knows, the softer the cloud form the less the wind, and when clouds are harder, more tufted, and more sharply outlined, the wind will be stronger. See WEATHER PREDICTING.

Collections. Things of the same kind, such as stones, shells, stamps, tree leaves, maps, pictures, or pennants which the Cub

Stamp collecting is a favorite hobby

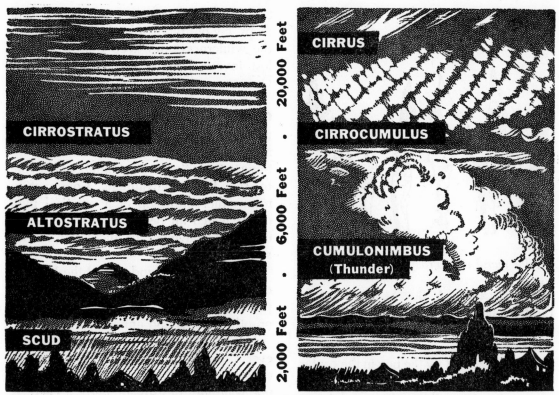

Typical cloud formations which Scouts learn to "read"

Scout has fun in collecting. Objects a boy may collect are almost without limit. Collections are started during Cub Scouting days which can be added to all during life and often become of great value.

The Cub Scout is encouraged to start a collection of his own. At first his private collection may be in his pocket. Once a Wolf Cub Scout took everything from his trouser's pocket and put the objects on a table. He had a bit of green glass, a fishhook, a top, a knife, four buttons, two marbles, and a frog!

These were all the things he wanted to collect. They did not mean much as a collection, and when his mother saw them she said:

"Now instead of collecting all these different things—and this frog! my goodness! —why don't you start a real collection of just one thing? These buttons, for instance,

could be the beginning. You could collect all kinds of buttons. There are bone buttons and pearl buttons and metal buttons. They come in round shapes, oval shapes, and square shapes, and in all sizes. You could have a fine collection."

So the Cub Scout is encouraged to choose something interesting, as well as something that will be fun. Instead of keeping his collection in a box or in a pile somewhere, he is urged to mount or use it in some appealing fashion.

For instance, a map collection can be used as interesting wallpaper. Nut shells can be strung on strings for a drapery. Christmas cards, pictures, and clippings can be placed neatly in an album. Valuable stamps are kept in an album, too, but some can be pasted on the back of a glass dish.

Boy Scouts make collections also, usually nature collections for school, the Troop

41

meeting room, or the Troop or camp museum. See CUB SCOUT.

Color guard with Troop and Council flags

Color Guard. A Boy Scout escort for the National Colors. Being a member of a Color Guard is a great honor. There are three or more boys in a Color Guard, the Flag being carried by the boy in the center. Color Guards are used at Unit and camp ceremonies, Council meetings, and in parades and on other occasions. See FLAG CODE.

Compass. An instrument for determining directions by means of a magnetic needle pointing to the north. The Boy

A compass shows the Scout his way

Scout with his compass can follow trail maps, lay out plots of land, find his way in the wilderness, and keep from becoming lost in any kind of country. See LOST!, ORIENTEERING.

Conservation. The wise use of natural resources such as minerals, soil, plants, and animals so that these resources will continue to serve the greatest number of people to the fullest advantage. Conservation means the setting-up of a practical plan under which all people may share in the use and enjoyment of these natural resources.

The Scout must understand the Balance of Nature, or the Web of Life, and how plants and animals live, each depending on other plants and animals for existence.

In the ninth point of the Scout Law is every Scout's promise to help America conserve her natural resources. "He does not wantonly destroy property." There is also a "Conservation Pledge."

There is a Merit Badge group in conservation, including Soil and Water Conservation, Forestry, and Wildlife Management. There is a special award, the Hornaday Award, to recognize Scouts who do outstanding work. Organizations which are prepared to help Scouts in conservation work include the U.S. Forest Service, the Soil Conservation Service, the Fish and Wildlife Service, and the National Parks Service. See BALANCE OF NATURE, FORESTS, GRASSLANDS, HORNADAY AWARD, MERIT BADGES, SOIL AND WATER CONSERVATION, WILDLIFE.

Conservation Pledge. As America's resources are a part of the heritage of every citizen, the Scout takes a "Conservation Pledge." He promises: "I give my pledge as an American to save and faithfully to defend from waste the natural resources of my country—its soil and minerals, its forests, water, and wildlife." See CONSERVATION, SCOUT OATH AND LAW.

Cooking (Outdoor). Cooking over an open fire or campfire. Whether it is a Patrol cooking its own meals, or one Scout preparing his food in outdoorsman's style, this is one of the most enjoyable games in Scouting.

Outdoor cooking requires skill. Securing the necessary pots, pans, and other utensils, not too few but not too many, and packing them one inside the other, together with food and seasonings, are important. A place for the fire must be selected where it cannot spread. The fire must not be large. Glowing coals are best.

The outdoor cook must constantly watch his food. Meat must be turned to brown evenly. Skillets and pots must be moved if the food is cooking too fast or burning. Food must be stirred regularly. Some foods are cooked slowly and others rapidly, and all must be seasoned properly. The Scout brings along his own appetite. See BARK UTENSILS, CAMPING (ADVENTURE), CAMPING (LONG-TERM), COOKING WITHOUT UTENSILS, FIRES.

Cooking without Utensils. Real pioneer or Indian-style cooking. It is surprising the number of things that can be cooked and the various ways by which they can be cooked without pots and skillets. Scouts learn how to make their own cooking gear out of native materials.

On broiling sticks the Boy Scout cooks hot dogs, steaks, chops, ham, and other meats. The sticks are cut from sweet-wood trees, such as the sugar maple and birch, or nut-bearing trees. The stick is run through the meat or fish and held over the glowing coals.

Broiling grills are made by fashioning a forked stick into a tennis-racket shape and interweaving it with smaller sticks of sweet wood. Meat and poultry also may be broiled on roasting spits, made from two crotched sticks set in the ground with a third stick stuck through the meat and laid across the crotches. The meat is

An improvised broiling grill

turned on the spit as it cooks. Steaks can be cooked by laying them directly on hardwood coals and turning them when one side is cooked.

On smooth, flat stone griddles the Scout can cook his bacon, eggs, and griddle cakes. The stone is placed on four other stones and a fire built beneath. Naturally it is brushed off before being used. Fish and steaks can be easily broiled on planks propped before the fire.

Mud or clay baking is a favorite way of cooking, and almost any kind of meat or vegetable can be cooked in this fashion. The food is enclosed in damp clay, placed in the fire, and covered with hot coals. Chickens, after being drawn, are cooked with the feathers on. When the clay is removed the feathers come with it, and the chicken is ready to eat.

Potatoes can be cooked in their jackets by burying them in hot coals. Ears of corn can be cooked in the same fashion, the husks being left on the ears. Corn can also be roasted by running a stick into the pithy part of the cob and holding the ear over the fire.

Scouts know that water can be boiled in paper or bark containers as long as the flames do not reach above the water line. Water can be heated in almost anything by dropping hot stones into it—the cooking method of the Indian stone boilers. See BARBECUE, BREAD ON A STICK, FOIL COOKERY, IMU, KABOB.

Cookouts. A practice event to perfect skill in outdoor cooking. Many times cookouts are held as a part of back-yard socials. See COOKING (OUTDOOR).

Council. See LOCAL COUNCIL.

Council Fire. A big ceremonial fire held at Council camps. Scouts gather in the bright light of the flames, sing songs, tell stories, and put on stunts and dramatic skits, often serious ceremonies. Some-

An evening council fire

times a Troop may hold its own Council fire at camp, or even indoors in winter before a fireplace or an electric fire.

Country Boys. See RURAL SCOUTING.

Country, Duty to. Part of the Scout Oath or Promise in which the Scout, on his honor, promises "To do my duty to God and my country." See SCOUT OATH AND LAW.

Courteous, A Scout Is. The fifth point of the Scout Law. It states: "A SCOUT IS COURTEOUS. He is polite to all, especially to women, children, old people, and the weak and helpless. He must not take pay for being helpful or courteous." See SCOUT OATH AND LAW.

Court of Honor. A public ceremony at which a Scout is awarded the badge of rank he has earned. This is usually held in the Scout's own Troop. Sometimes, for higher ranks, there is a large District or Council Court of Honor ceremony.

Parents, Scoutmaster, and members of the Scout's Troop are present at the Court of Honor, and the badge is presented to the Scout in their presence. See ADVANCEMENT, BRIDGE OF HONOR.

Cracker Barrel. Scout lingo for a gabfest and refreshment session after a meeting.

Crew. A small group of Explorers in any Explorer Unit, corresponding to a Patrol in a Troop. A Crew is made up of two or more Explorers held together by a common interest. It elects its own officers. Two or more Crews make an Explorer Unit.

A Crew may also be formed by Explorers in a Boy Scout Troop, where they thus have the advantage of both Troop and Exploring programs. Among Sea Explorers, Crews are working teams like "watches" in oldtime sailing ships. See EXPLORER POST, SHIP (SEA EXPLORER).

Crew Leader. Leader of an Explorer Crew, elected by the Crew members. He leads the Crew members in following their own special interests and in contributing to the program of the entire Unit. See CREW.

Cruising. Water trips taken by Sea Explorers as a part of their program. Cruises are the ambition and aim of all Sea Explorers. They cruise along coastal waters and in the large inland lakes, as well as in rivers, creeks, and bayous. All cruises are conducted under the Sea Explorer Advisor's supervision. See SEA EXPLORER.

Cubmaster. Adult leader of a Cub Scout Pack. He knows how to teach games and songs, handicrafts and stunts. He is a fine man and Cub Scouts admire him. The Cubmaster works directly with the Den Mother, Den Chief, and Den Dad. He plans the programs for both the Den and the Pack. He is helped by Assistant Cubmasters. See CUB SCOUT, DEN, PACK.

Cub Scout. When a boy is eight, nine, or ten years old, he can become a Cub Scout, a registered member of the Boy Scouts of America, entitled to wear the Cub Scout uniform.

The Cub Scouting program is entirely different from Boy Scouting, because it takes place in or around the Cub Scout's home, neighborhood, or back yard. The Cub Scout plays games with the members of his Den. His Den Mother and Den Chief lead the Den. The Cub Scout learns how to make such things as model boats, kites, wagons, Indian costumes, and other handicraft objects. He also learns such interesting activities as boxing, rowing, and writing in secret codes.

Cub Scouting is a program for families, and not merely for boys. The Cub Scout's mother and dad are in Cub Scouting, too.

Cub Scouts make and fly model kites

They help their son advance in his work and they are present when he receives his badges.

The boy first becomes a Bobcat and receives a Bobcat Badge which he wears on his civilian clothes. To earn this badge, he must learn to give the Cub Scout Promise, repeat the Law of the Pack, and tell what it means. He must tell what Webelos means, show the Cub Scout Sign and Handshake, and explain what they mean. Finally he must give the Cub Scout Motto and Salute and tell what both mean.

After this a Bobcat can become a Wolf Cub Scout by doing the twelve Wolf achievements, or the twelve things he needs to do in following the Wolf Trail. These include feats of skill, saluting the Flag of the United States, handling tools, making collections, cooking, swimming, and other things.

45

The next rank is that of Bear Cub Scout, which he may reach when he is nine. When he is ten, the Cub Scout can earn the higher rank of Lion Cub Scout, and when he is ten and a half, he earns his Webelos rank, the highest rank in Cub Scouting. When he is eleven, he graduates and becomes a Tenderfoot Scout in a Boy Scout Troop.

The Cub Scout joins a Pack, which meets once a month. The Pack is made up of Dens, each of which meets one afternoon a week in the back yard or other convenient place of one of the Cub Scouts. An older Cub Scout, a Denner, is leader of the Den and he is helped by an Assistant Denner.

The Den Chief is a Boy Scout or Explorer. He leads the Cub Scouts in their games and handicrafts and helps the Den Mother run the Den. The office of Den Chief is one of high honor, and to serve as Den Chief is to do one of the finest Good Turns a Boy Scout can perform.

The Pack is led by a man, a Cubmaster. See BEAR CUB SCOUT, BOBCAT, CUBMASTER, CUB SCOUT PROMISE AND LAW, DEN, DEN CHIEF, DEN DAD, DEN MOTHER, DENNER, LION, PACK, TENDERFOOT SCOUT, WEBELOS, WOLF.

1. *Bobcat Badge*
2. *Wolf Cub Badge*
3. *Bear Cub Badge*
4. *Lion Cub Badge*

Cub Scout Promise and Law. The first thing that a Bobcat, or new Cub Scout, does is to learn to give the Cub Scout Promise:

"I, (name), promise to DO MY BEST to do my DUTY TO GOD and my COUNTRY, to be SQUARE and to OBEY the Law of the Pack."

Then he must learn the Law of the Pack:

"The Cub Scout FOLLOWS Akela.
The Cub Scout HELPS the Pack go.
The Pack HELPS the Cub Scout grow.
The Cub Scout GIVES good will."

In his own words the Cub Scout then explains what the Law of the Pack means. See AKELA, CUB SCOUT.

Deadman. A type of ground anchor. Sometimes a log, with a rope or cable tied to its middle part, is buried in the ground at right angles to the object it is to hold. A deadman is used as an anchorage to a Monkey Bridge. See BRIDGES.

A deadman is a ground anchor

Democracy. The Scout Patrol has been called the smallest democracy, because it operates under a boy leader chosen by his "peers," the Scouts in the Patrol. There are other boy leaders in the Patrol elected in the same way.

The Scout uniform teaches democracy. Sons of rich men and boys who earn their own living are all on the same basis in the uniform. Everybody does his share of work in a Scout camp in the democratic fashion. The Scout learns to stand on his own feet and earn what money he needs for his Scouting expenses, instead of waiting for a handout. He studies the democratic principles on which America is based in his Citizenship Merit Badges. Scouting is open to all boys of very race and religious belief, just as America welcomes all on a democratic basis. See BOY SCOUT, CITIZENSHIP, PATROL.

Den. A small neighborhood group of Cub Scouts. A Den is made up of from two to eight boys who live near one another and play together. The mother of one of the Cub Scouts is Den Mother. She helps with their games, hobbies, and other activities, together with a Den Chief and a Denner. Dens meet every week or oftener. A Cub Pack is made up of Dens. See CUB SCOUT, DEN CHIEF, PACK.

Den Chief. A Boy Scout or Explorer who leads the Cub Scouts in their games and handicraft work in a Den and helps the Den Mother. The Den Chief is a big brother or friend, but never a boss. The office of Den Chief is a high honor for a Boy Scout. He is a hero to the smaller boys. See CUB SCOUT, DEN, DEN MOTHER.

Den Dad. The father of a Cub Scout, who helps the Den. He also encourages other fathers to become interested in father-and-son activities.

A Den Dad usually serves on the Pack Committee where he represents the parents of the boys in his own Den. See Cub Scout, Den.

Den Mother. Mother of a Cub Scout in whose back yard or home the Den meets. The Den Mother's badge and uniform are blue and gold. She arranges the Den program; shows the Cub Scouts how to make toys, models, kites, and other things; teaches them games and songs; and helps them dress up to play circus or give a show. She's full of fun and sparkle and the boys love her. The Den Chief and Denner help her run the Den. See Cub Scout, Den, Den Chief.

Denner. A Cub Scout leader of the Den. He is selected by the Cub Scouts. He leads the Den between the weekly meetings, helps the Den Chief and Den Mother, and has other duties which she assigns to him. See Cub Scout, Den, Den Chief, Den Mother.

Scouts find adventure in deserts

Desert Living. By learning to live in the desert the Scout finds many interesting nature adventures. Through his knowledge of desert secrets he is able to survive under conditions in which most people believe plants and animals, as well as man, cannot live.

Deserts are usually places where most plants cannot thrive, either because of cold or because of dryness. Drought deserts are sunny, hot, and dry. Cold deserts are high mountain icefields. In the United States there are five different kinds of deserts: *cold desert* (mountain tops); *northern desert-shrub* (sagebrush); *southern desert-shrub* (creosote bush); *desert grass-savanna* (mesquite grasslands); *salt desert-shrub* (greasewood).

Making smoke signals

Distress Signals. There are times when a Scout may need to recognize or send distress signals. By spelling out "SOS" with the Morse Code he can send such a signal with auto headlights at night or with smoke puffs and mirror flashes during the day.

A flag flown upside down is an old-time distress signal. Riding a pony around in small circles, or running in small circles on the crest of a bluff or in view of help, also is a distress signal. A cowboy waves his hat from right to left and back, and Indians flashed mirrors in the same fashion. Three shots in the air means a call for help. See Signals.

Ditty Bag. A small bag carried at the top of a pack. In the ditty bag are things needed along the trail, such as fishline and hooks, wire, pliers, needles and thread, extra flashlight bulbs, and batteries. See PACKS (FOR CARRYING).

Dogs. The dog has been called "the whistler's friend." This loyal and trusting animal is always ready to come at the call of his young master. The boy and his dog are two things always thought of together.

A Scout knows how to care for his dog

Almost the earliest human beings of whom there is any record seem to have been accompanied by dogs. Dogs apparently were among the first animals domesticated. The dog has been termed "man's best friend," and poets have sung his praises. Lord Byron in "An Inscription to a Newfoundland Dog," wrote:

"The poor dog, in life the firmest friend,
The first to welcome, foremost to defend."

Some fifty years ago George Graham Vest, in defending a dog in a Missouri court, said:

"The only absolutely unselfish friend that a man can have in this selfish world, the one that never proves ungrateful or treach-

erous, is his dog. A man's dog stands by him in poverty, in health, and in sickness."

The Scout loves and cares for his dog. He learns the best methods of bathing and grooming him, what to feed him, and how often. He practices first aid to animals, in case his pet should be injured.

Scouts help local humane societies. They distribute leaflets, give talks to schoolchildren about kindness to animals, and in many ways help all dogs have happier lives. Two Merit Badge subjects, First Aid to Animals and Dog Care, help Scouts to learn how to care for dogs. See MERIT BADGES.

"Do Your Best." Cub Scout Motto and daily reminder. It means that when a Cub Scout plays a game, studies in school or helps at home, he does his best. Other boys may do better, but so long as the Cub Scout does his best, he need not be ashamed. In Canada, Wolf Cubs use the initials for a kind of yell. "Cubs," says the leader, "dyb!" "We'll dyb, dyb, dyb!" reply the Cubs.

Duffel. A Scout's outfit or trail supplies. Duffel is carried in a duffel bag and includes sleeping gear, first aid kit, personal kit, food, cooking gear, and extra clothes. The duffel bag is best carried on a pack frame or harness. See PACK FRAMES.

Dutch-Oven Cooking. Baking or roasting in an iron pot or other metal container. The Dutch oven is raised on legs attached to the pot. Hot coals are placed beneath and also heaped on the lid.

Duty to God. The Scout's duty to God is a part of his Scout Promise, and his reverence toward God is the twelfth point of the Scout Law. See SCOUT OATH AND LAW.

49

Eagle Scout. As the Scout stands before the Court of Honor to receive his badge of Eagle rank, his parents, his Scoutmaster, and members of his Troop look on proudly.

This Scout has climbed the trail to the highest rank in Scouting. It is a fine moment in his life and the lives of those near and dear to him when he receives the cherished badge—the recognition of his achievements.

The Eagle Scout Badge

The Eagle Badge carries great prestige. It is awarded to those who are physically strong, mentally awake, and morally straight; to those Scouts who are self-reliant, who accept responsibility and leadership in the Troop, who give service to their homes, churches, schools and communities; who are good outdoorsmen.

The Eagle Scout has earned twenty-one Merit Badges to equip him to be of service to others, to stand on his own feet, and to do his share as a future citizen.

These Merit Badges are selected by the Scout from certain required groups. One Badge must be from the Conservation group, three from the Citizenship group, one from the Outdoor group, and one from any of the following groups: Animal Husbandry, Plant Cultivation, Communication, Transportation, Building.

Certain other Merit Badges are required for Eagle rank so that the Scout may be better equipped to take care of others and himself: Camping, Cooking, Swimming, Life Saving, Nature, Personal Fitness, Public Health, Safety, Firemanship, First Aid.

The Scout must serve at least six months as a Life Scout.

The Eagle is the highest rank in Scouting. Explorers also may qualify. The Scout wears his Eagle Badge suspended from the flap of the left breast pocket of his uniform to the right of all other badges, except only the Gold Honor Medal. See ADVANCEMENT, COURT OF HONOR, LIFE SCOUT, MERIT BADGES.

The Scout stands proudly before the Court of Honor to receive his Eagle Badge

Emergency Service. In hundreds of emergencies and times of disaster, such as earthquakes, hurricanes, floods, and fires, Scouts have given outstanding aid to local authorities, the Red Cross, and the nation. They have carried messages, acted as guides, routed traffic, helped pass out supplies of food and clothing, given first aid, and helped in rescue operations.

In the Emergency Service Plan of the Boy Scouts of America, every Explorer and Explorer Unit is expected to train to mobilize for effective service in time of emergency and disaster. See EXPLORER.

Expedition. A high adventure enjoyed by an Explorer Unit at least once a year when it sets out on a wilderness trip. This is Exploring in action. The young men do not usually follow beaten trails, and may hike with packs on their backs or use

horses, bicycles, canoes, or motorboats. See SURVIVAL TECHNIQUES.

Explorer. A registered boy member of the Boy Scouts of America, fourteen years of age or older. The Boy Scout on his fourteenth birthday automatically becomes an Explorer; any young man of fourteen can become an Explorer by joining a Boy Scout Troop or Explorer Post, Ship, or Squadron. If there are no Troops or Explorer Units in his neighborhood, he may become a Lone Explorer.

No matter which kind of Unit he joins, within the Unit the young man belongs to a Crew. The members of the Crew have the same interests—fishing, boating, photography, aviation, mechanics, or whatever it may be.

The Crew, composed of two to eight members, is a working team. On expeditions or cruises, the Crew travels together, camps and stands watches together. They work together on community projects and get together for social hours.

Explorers themselves are responsible for planning their own programs and meetings. In this way, each Explorer has a share. The Explorer Advisor guides and helps them when needed. Each Crew has a Crew Leader and his Assistant. There is a Senior Crew Leader for the Unit.

Explorer uniforms vary in color according to the program. Air Explorers wear horizon blue; Sea Explorers, navy blue; Explorers in Posts have a choice of khaki Scout uniforms or forest green. There is a fatigue uniform common to all three.

Explorer activities include outdoor programs such as expeditions, regattas, cruises, outdoor sports, and camping; social gatherings, often with girls, such as dances, hay or sleigh rides, roller or ice skating, picnics; community service such as conservation work, emergency service practice, and other helpful projects; and indoor meetings, including vocational and hobby exploration, debates, putting on plays, and other interesting activities. These are planned by four Program Committees, each of which specializes in one phase of the Unit's program.

Explorers subscribe to the Scout Oath and Law and abide by the principles of Scouting.

When a Scout reaches fourteen, he may prefer to remain in his Troop instead of joining an outside Explorer Unit. In that case, he and other young men may form an Explorer Crew in the Troop, and have the advantage of both the Troop and Explorer programs. He probably has a leadership position in the Troop as Patrol Leader, Junior Assistant Scoutmaster (at sixteen), or instructor. See AIR EXPLORER, BOY SCOUT, EAGLE SCOUT, SEA EXPLORER.

Explorer Advisor. A mature man who is appointed by the Explorer Unit Committee to lead an Explorer Unit. He is just what his name indicates—an advisor. Programs are developed by Explorers themselves with the active counsel of the Advisor. The Advisor attends all meetings of the Unit and, with the Unit Committee, is responsible for the general program and supervision of the Unit. See EXPLORER.

Explorer Post. An Explorer Unit of not less than five Explorers and an Explorer Advisor, which specializes in land activities like wilderness camping, vocational exploration, and expeditions. Posts are made up of two or more Crews. Members of an Explorer Post may wear a uniform of forest green, or the Scout or Scouter uniform. See EXPLORER.

Explorer Silver Award. The highest recognition in Exploring. It is given only by the National Council of the Boy Scouts upon recommendation of the Explorer's leaders and the Council. To earn the Silver Award, an Explorer in a Troop or Post must show growth in leadership ability, social development, understanding of citizenship responsibility on a national and international plane, and have four Explorer ratings. See EXPLORER.

An Explorer Post prepares for a hike into the wilderness

Father-and-Son Hike. A special event when fathers and their Scout sons get together. A favorite time is Father's Day in June when fathers are invited for a day with their sons in the Troop or Patrol camp. Special games and contests are held in which fathers and sons take part together, a camp supper is prepared, and the day ends with campfire ceremonies. See CAMP-FIRE CEREMONIES.

Federal Charter. A Federal charter was granted by Congress to the Boy Scouts of America on June 15, 1916. The charter protects the name and insignia of the organization and authorizes the Scout uniform so that none but Scouts can wear it. See BOY SCOUTS OF AMERICA.

Field Signals. An observer, watching a group of Scouts moving about a field—now lining up in single formation, now moving into a perfect circle, and, after forming into an open column, marching off—scratched his head in wonderment.

There had been no shouted commands or whistle blown, yet the Scouts had gone through their formations without a hitch, as if commanded by some secret voice.

"They must all have some of those new-fangled radio receivers in their pockets," commented the observer. "They are being directed by radio."

"No, just watch that fellow over there on the edge of the field," said a man nearby. "Watch his arms."

Scouts use Field Signals for Troop drills

This leader was, in fact, making signals with his arms and hands. He now raised his arms, bent at the elbows, fists doubled and held vertically. At this signal the Patrols closed up their marching columns.

The Scouts were being directed by Field Signals, the same kind of silent signals used by Indians during buffalo hunts or surrounds, and also when in the presence of the enemy. No wonder the man watching the Scouts was puzzled at how quickly the groups formed, marched off, and came to a halt.

Field Signals, known as Trail Signals when used on the trail or in games of stalking, or whenever silence is necessary, are also used for other games and for assemblies for a parade. While Scouts find a certain amount of drill necessary for getting Troop and Patrols into position for various activities, and for moving the Troop in an orderly manner, this is not a military drill and is considered more as a game.

In the Troop meeting room, too, the Leader raises his right hand in the Scout Sign high above his head when he wants to indicate "Attention," "Silence," or "I have an announcement to make." Instantly there is quiet. This signal, known as the Alert Signal, also is employed on other occasions as the signal to "freeze," or become instantly immovable, no matter what the Scout is doing. See SIGNALS.

Fingerprinting. A means of individual identification by taking impressions of the ridge formations on the inside of the "bulb," or nail joint, of the finger. No two fingers have ever been found where the patterns of these ridges are the same.

Taking a thumb print

Scouts can earn a Merit Badge in fingerprinting. In this they render valuable aid to the Federal Bureau of Identification (FBI), as one of the requirements for the badge is the obtaining of fingerprints of five persons and showing that they have been accepted for the Civil Identification files of the FBI. This file, established by J. Edgar Hoover, is separate from the records of the criminal division. See MERIT BADGES.

Fire Building. How to start a fire, the kind of wood to use, the type of fire to build in wet or dry weather, and finally how to put out a fire are things

Building a tepee fire

every Second Class Scout learns. With the proper fire the Scout can cook his food, warm his shelter, and hold his campfire ceremonies when dusk comes.

The type of fire depends upon what it is to be used for, and the location. Let us watch a Scout build a commonly used fire, the *tepee fire.* Having arrived at his campsite, he first unpacks his gear. It is only the Tenderfoot who first builds a fire and then unpacks.

For his fire the Scout picks a spot in the open at least ten feet away from any brush and near a fuel supply. He is careful not to select one beneath the overhanging branches of a tree. He now clears a circle six feet in diameter, removing all dry leaves, brush, or other material which might cause his fire to spread. He scoops out a hollow in the ground.

He gathers his kindling and firewood, bringing in enough firewood to last the length of the fire. The kindling may consist of shredded pine cones, tops of dead weeds, birch wood, dead evergreen branches or pine needles, or a roll of birch bark or cedar

A reflector fire is best for baking

bark from a dead tree. It must always be dry. A big handful is needed. His firewood consists of small dead branches, gathered from the ground or broken from a tree. These are from pencil-thickness to thumb-thickness in size. The Indians call them "squaw wood."

The Scout now wets his finger, holds it up, and determines the direction of the wind. This is very important. With his back to the wind he arranges his kindling, stacking it in pyramid or tepee form. Then on the side away from the wind he leans thin pieces of firewood.

He strikes his match, cups it in his hands until the flame is licking along the stick, and lights his kindling close to the ground, on the side from which the wind is coming. After the kindling has caught, he begins to feed his firewood on the lee side—the side

away from the wind. He uses small sticks first and then larger ones.

When the fire is blazing, the Scout uses it for boiling. He arranges his dingle stick— a stick anchored in the ground at one end and slanting upward over the fire. On the end he hangs his pot. Flames for boiling, coals or embers for broiling, is the rule.

There are several types of fires. The Scout may build a fireplace. He may have a *reflector fire* for baking or for throwing the heat in one direction. Reflectors can be made of logs, stones, or mud. He may use a fire in a hole or a *trench fire*. The *hunter's* or *trapper's fire* is built between two logs. The *council* or *camp powwow fire* is built from crisscross logs.

In any case, after the Scout has started his fire, he remains near it. He watches it at all times. He knows that it is criminal to leave a fire unattended, and when he leaves camp, if only for a short time, he puts it out. When he moves camp, he is sure his fire is extinguished, and he leaves his Scout mark to show this—two crossed sticks on the place where his fire has been. See FIRE BY FRICTION; FIRE, HOW TO PUT OUT A; FIREPLACES.

Fire by Friction. Picture a scene where a small group is isolated in some fashion in the primitive wilds. It is cold and there is no way of getting warm. There is food, but no way to cook it.

Such a scene may seem a remote possibility, yet in this day of aviation when men cross great expanses of uninhabited territory, perhaps not so remote.

Fire is necessary to man. And a Scout can make fire without matches, without a burning glass, even without flint and steel. He is trained to make fire by friction, by the most ancient method known to man, by what is commonly termed "rubbing two sticks together."

Yet fire by friction is not so simple as the mere rubbing of two sticks together. It requires skill, and the Scout, an expert in outdoor crafts, has such skill.

The Scout first selects his spindle or drill, measuring its length as halfway to his knee. It is of a dry, seasoned wood, without resin. He next fashions a bow from a stick with a slight curve in it, and strings this stick loosely with a thong of leather or softened rawhide or a stout cord. He makes a thunderbird, or socket, from a block of hard wood slightly larger than his hand, and digs a small hole in its center. He finds a flat piece of dry wood, maybe elm, willow, white poplar, or possibly yucca. This is his fire board, or hearth. In the hearth he gouges out a small hole near the edge and cuts a v-shaped notch to the very edge,

The Scout can make fire without matches

with the point of the v almost at the center of the hole. He must now have tinder, and perhaps he carries with him some charred linen or cotton cloth. If not, he pounds some dry cedar bark to a pulp, rolls it in his hands to rid it of the hard, grainy part, and makes it into a nest.

He places this at the wide end of the v.

The anxious moment is at hand. The Scout sets his drill in the hole or cup of the fire board, gives a turn of the bowstring around the drill, and to provide pressure, hooks his left arm around his knee with the left foot holding down the fire board. Then he begins long, regular strokes with his bow, back and forth, back and forth.

The drill spins in the cup and soon smoke arises. Hot, minute bits of sawdust collect and form a small ember. A tiny fire is being born. The Scout nurses it, blows on it, works it into his tinder which is cupped over, and soon there is a flicker of a flame!

The description is long, but fire-making by this ancient method is brief when done by trained hands. It has been accomplished in six seconds! See FIRE BUILDING.

Fire Drill. Schoolteachers often call on Scouts to help in safety work, especially at fire drills. The Scout training in leadership in emergencies is valuable, and in performing these duties the Scout is doing one of his Daily Good Turns. See GOOD TURN.

Fire, How to Put out a. One of the most important lessons learned by the Scout is how to put out a fire. The last ember must be extinguished. The Scout does not pour water on a fire but sprinkles it until the flames are out, and then spreads out the smoking sticks and sprinkles them till they are soaked. Sand, gravel, loose earth, or rocks can be used when no water is available. When the fire is completely out, he marks the place with crossed sticks to show that he left the fire completely out. See FIRES AND FIREMANSHIP.

Fireplaces. Fireplaces are used for campfires for several reasons. One is safety, to keep a fire from spreading. Another is so that the fire will be small, hot, and concen-

57

trated for cooking. Still another is so the fire will throw heat in one direction for warmth.

A fire in a hole is good for windy or treeless country. Fires in trenches are good for cooking. Fireplaces can be built of stones, with larger stones or earth-covered logs for reflectors. The fireplace can be elevated by piling up stones or logs and, if made of logs, by covering the top with earth. This is an altar fire, and in using it the cook does not have to lean over. See FIRE BUILDING.

Fire Prevention. Whether in camp or at home, the Scout is always on the alert to prevent fires that may damage forests or property. He uses every precaution in seeing that his campfire does not spread and that it is completely out when he leaves camp. In his community he co-operates with the fire department and is always on the lookout for fire hazards. See FIRES AND FIREMANSHIP.

Quick action puts out a fire

Fires and Firemanship. A wise man once said: "A match has a head but no brains. When you use *its* head, use *your* brains." Carelessness with matches and smoking materials; misuse of electricity; defective chimneys and flues; faulty stoves, furnaces, and pipes; and spontaneous igni-

tion have been found to be the principal causes of home fires in this country. There are many other causes, of course.

Good firemanship means not only preventing fires but fighting fires. In the city there is the organized fire department. In the country and rural districts fires become individual or community problems.

In qualifying for a Firemanship Merit Badge the Scout learns that in country homes it becomes necessary to provide some sort of equipment for fighting fires—a hand-pump tank or a fire extinguisher.

The Scout is always on the lookout to prevent fires. He watches for improper storage of flammable materials and is prepared to aid in extinguishing neighborhood fires. See FIRE PREVENTION, MERIT BADGES.

First Aid. A small boy ran up to a group of older boys. He was excited, out of breath, and could hardly speak.

"A man—a man—he fell off a ladder—he's hurt!" he blurted out.

"Come on, let's go. Where is he?" asked one of the older boys.

"Over there, in that lot. He was working on a high fence," said the younger boy.

"Let's go!"

"I'll get the doctor," offered the younger boy, starting off.

"No, you come along with us. Then we'll send for the doctor."

The boys ran at top speed toward the lot. There they saw a man on the ground at the foot of a ladder. He was on his back and appeared to be unconscious.

The older boy, who had taken charge of the situation, kneeled down and began carefully to examine the man. He felt all over him and loosened his clothing.

"Better get a doctor," said the younger boy.

"Yes, you run as fast as you can and get the doctor. Tell him this man has a head

Prompt first aid may save a life

injury—he hurt his head. No cuts. Bring the doctor back the nearest way."

As the younger boy dashed off, the other boys gathered around. The man opened his eyes and blinked. He started to get up.

"What happened?" he murmured.

"You fell. Just stay still. Don't try to get up," cautioned the boy beside him.

"I'm all right—just a little bump on the head. Gee, my head hurts." The man sank back. "I'm okay, though. I'll just get up and walk about a bit—"

"No, you just stay still. The doctor will be here in a minute."

"Doctor? Who are you?"

"I'm a Scout—just happened to be nearby. I think you'd better lie down and take it easy."

"Scout, eh? Oh, then you must know what you are talking about. Okay, son, I'll wait for the doctor."

The doctor soon came. The Scout explained the situation in a few words. The doctor examined the man, felt his pulse, and looked into his eyes.

"There wasn't much to do, my boy," he said, "but you did exactly the right thing. You kept him quiet. This man probably has a slight concussion."

The Scout had been taught that all injuries, except those which are so simple that they can be treated as minor injuries, must be considered major injuries. That is the safe way to look at it. He knew that a major injury was probably attended by shock.

First aid is treatment given by someone trained to help in emergencies while waiting for a physician. The Scout is prepared to give immediate first aid in emergency cases such as poisoning, severe bleeding, or asphyxiation. He can administer artificial respiration in cases of electric shock or drowning, or in asphyxiation resulting from gas fumes.

He can apply a tourniquet or stop bleeding by pressure of his fingers on certain parts of the body. He can apply splints on fractures, bandages on sprains, and give immediate relief for burns and minor injuries. When a person must be moved out of danger, or when he can be removed without further injury to himself, the Scout knows the proper type of carry, or the method of transporting him. He knows the patient should never be moved unless absolutely necessary. Always he sends for a doctor if it is possible.

All Scouts learn first aid, and there is a Merit Badge for advanced skill. See ARTIFICIAL RESPIRATION, BANDAGING, CARRIES, MERIT BADGES.

First Aid Kits. An interesting and useful project for Scouts and Explorers is the making of first aid kits for their Unit and for home and personal use. The Unit kit may be a portable one to be used as a community first aid emergency outfit.

The home first aid kit is similar to the Unit kit, the chief difference being that the number of separate items is smaller. Most homes have nearly all of the items scattered here and there, and the Scout brings them together in one place. The personal kit can be made of a tobacco can, typewriter-ribbon box, or plastic cigarette case. It contains a one-inch roller bandage, one-inch adhesive tape, Band-Aids, antiseptic, safety pins, razor blade, Halazone tablets, soap, two-inch-square sterile pads, and other small items. See FIRST AID.

First Class Scout. The third rank in Scouting. The boy advances to this from Second Class rank by showing improvement in the three important requirements of Scout Spirit, Scout Participation, and Scoutcraft. By going on hikes he has improved his cooking and his ability to use his axe. By observation and tracking he has

The First Class Scout receives his badge

learned more about nature. Camping, swimming, signaling, advanced mapping, compass work, and nature study are among the First Class requirements. The First Class Scout Badge, which is the trefoil and scroll combined, is usually awarded at a Troop Court of Honor, which parents and friends attend. See SCOUT BADGE, SCOUTCRAFT, SCOUT PARTICIPATION, SCOUT SPIRIT, SECOND CLASS SCOUT.

Fish and Wildlife Service. A branch of the Department of the Interior, dealing with wildlife problems and conservation. The main offices are located at 200 North Jefferson Street, Chicago, Illinois.

Fishes. Backboned animals which live in water, breathe by means of gills, and have paired fins. There are thousands and thousands of kinds of fishes, inhabiting waters from the smallest streams to the largest oceans. The Scout learns the species of fish in his part of the country, their feeding habits, and those which are good to eat. Many Troops help the game wardens or the conservation commission in "planting" young fish or building dams to provide feeding and resting places. See FISHING.

Fishing (Angling). A popular Scout sport. The Scout learns to catch fish by the usual angling methods such as fly-casting, trolling, and bait-casting.

In camp he learns to construct fish traps and make emergency fishhooks of bone, quills, and hardwood slivers. He can fashion a fishline from basswood bark, and construct barbed fishing spears. All laws protecting fish are carefully observed by the Scout. See FISHES.

Flag Code. A code officially adopted in a joint resolution by Congress on December 22, 1942, for the display of the Flag of the United States. Forms of respect to the Flag, and the manner in which the Flag should be displayed are part of this code. Every Scout learns this part of the Flag Code in his Tenderfoot requirements. See PLEDGE OF ALLEGIANCE.

Designs for Patrol flags are varied

Flags. Each Patrol has its flag, with the Patrol totem displayed on it. Each Troop has its flag, also, showing its number with the Scout Badge and the Council name.

The flag goes wherever the Troop or Patrol goes. Some Patrols make their own flags. The flagpole may be decorated with streamers or carved designs. Scouts are proud of their flags, and they make a colorful picture when the Troop marches off on a hike or to camp. Of course, each Troop also has its own United States Flag.

Flapjacks. There is more to flapjacks than just eating them. There is the pleas-

Flipping the flapjack

ure of flipping them over in the air and catching them again in the pan to cook them on the other side.

To make flapjacks, mix 1 cupful of flour, ½ teaspoon of salt, 1 heaping teaspoon of baking powder. Add water or milk slowly, mixing the dough into a thin batter that flows easily. Grease the pan and pour in the batter. When bubbles cover the top of the flapjack, flip it!

Flowering Plants. Plants that blossom. The Scout can quickly recognize plants by their flowers. He is no wild-flower picker and leaves the blooming plants in their places to be admired by others. However, he knows that in emergencies certain plants are good for eating. The flowers, as well as the young shoots, of the milkweed are an example. Jerusalem artichokes, a type of

61

wild sunflower, produce delicious underground parts that may be eaten raw or cooked. Sunflower seeds are good, too. Indians were fond of rosebuds as well as the flowers of grasses and other plants. See WILD FOODS.

Foil Cookery. The use of aluminum foil instead of pots or pans in cooking. Meat and potatoes, for instance, can be cooked by wrapping them in a double thickness of foil and placing on the coals. Anything that can be cooked in ordinary vessels can be cooked in foil. See COOKING WITHOUT UTENSILS.

Food Bags. Bags for carrying food must be waterproof, dust-proof, and grease-proof. The Scout makes good ones from old salt and sugar bags or other handy cloth. He rubs paraffin wax into the weave of the cloth and smooths it with a warm iron. Some food bags are made from plastic cloth.

Forestry. Scouts plant millions of trees each year to help conservation. These are set out with the advice of conservation leaders on campsites, or on public property. These trees help prevent soil erosion, provide food for wild life, or future timber. They add beauty to the scenery and value to property. Scouts not only help their country, but have fun in this worth-while project. They also help preserve forests by preventing forest fires and working with fire wardens in putting out fires. They serve as lookouts and forest rangers. See CONSERVATION, FORESTS, FOREST SERVICE.

Forestry Camps. Camps established during the summer in state and national forests where Scout and Explorer groups render service to the forestry program. Explorers work four hours a day, for which they draw pay. They help in road building, trail marking, and in nurseries. The remainder of each day is devoted to Scout activities. In at least one camp for Eagle Scouts near Boulder Junction, Wisconsin, the Scouts are employed by the state, with the privilege of camping in the forests. See CONSERVATION, FORESTS, MERIT BADGES.

Forests. Large sections of land where trees and underbrush grow thickly. There are several different kinds of forests, with different types of trees, wildlife, insects, and birds. Over thirty million people visit National Forests yearly, and millions more visit forests in National Parks. Scouts go camping in forests, and often help to maintain them. Conservation and reforestation are projects successfully carried out by many Units. Some forests today are being wooded scientifically by city, state, and national governments, as well as by private interests. See CONSERVATION, FORESTRY.

Forest Service. A service devoted to the development and conservation of forests. At present there are about six thousand foresters and several thousand forest range riders, forestry specialists, and rangers employed by city, state, and national governments. See CONSERVATION, FORESTRY.

Friendly, A Scout Is. The fourth point in the Scout Law. "A SCOUT IS FRIENDLY. He is a friend to all and a brother to every other Scout." The world-wide Scout Brotherhood is based on friendship. Scouts go to different churches, they may be rich or poor, have different-colored skins and different languages, but in Scouting all are friends. See SCOUT OATH AND LAW.

Forestry in action—Scouts plant millions of trees each year

Galley. The ship's kitchen. A term used in Sea Exploring. See Sea Explorer.

Games. One of the reasons why Scouting, Cub Scouting, and Exploring are such fun is that games are enjoyed at many meetings. Some of these games involve Scouting skills, and all are played for pleasure. Outdoor games are a feature of hikes, camp activities, and campfires.

Cub Scouts play quiet games at indoor Den meetings and more active games in the outdoors and in Pack meetings. Boy Scouts enjoy every variety of active playground game. At some part of their meetings time is set aside for a game period, generally toward the end of the meetings. Explorers not only enjoy the nature study and treasure hunt type of "wide" game played at camp, but they also like to play more or less difficult versions of Scout games with strenuous competition. Party games are popular at co-ed affairs.

Here are some of the different types of games played by Scout groups:

Circle games
Around-the-table games (Dens)
Dual tests of strength and skill
Tag games
Nature study games (hikes)
Boat and canoe races (camp)
Campfire games
Relay and novelty races
Balloon games
Opposed-line games
"Scout Advancement" games
Water sports and stunts
Stalking and cross-country games (camp)
Party games (Explorer parties)

Here is a stalking game called "Treasure Train," very popular with Scouts in camp.

The players are divided into two parties, Cowboys and Bandits, with a Sheriff and a Bandit Chief in charge of each group, respectively. The Cowboys receive fairly definite sealed directions as to the location of the "treasure," and try to bring it back to headquarters, which is now picketed by Bandits at least one hundred yards away. Some of the Bandits also advance toward the treasure train to attack.

The treasure is some object previously known which is too large to conceal. Both Bandits and Cowboys wear colored yarn on their left arms, each party having a distinguishing color. A battle may ensue, each trying to pull off the enemy's yarn. If a man loses his yarn, he is out of the game. The Bandits win if they intercept the treasure. The Cowboys win if they get through. If the treasure is not brought in within a

Scouts like Indian wrestling

reasonable time, the director may give the Cowboys ten minutes to get it in or lose the game.

After the treasure is sighted, it is permissible for the Bandits to close in up to within fifty paces of the headquarters.

Gardening. It was early in April. The Scouts of Troop 7 were meeting by Patrols in the Patrol dens in the corners of the Troop meeting room. The Patrol Leader was talking to the Scouts of the Beaver Patrol.

"Now you've all heard what the Scoutmaster told us," he said. "The Secretary of Agriculture in Washington has asked all Troops to continue their Liberty Gardens this year, because there is still need to grow extra food supplies and will be for many years to come. 'Liberty Gardens' he calls the project. We've got to vote on whether we want to raise a Liberty Garden again this year."

"Sam," said a Scout, "some of the new fellows don't know about what we did last year. Why don't you tell them?"

"Well, fellows," said the Patrol Leader, "the Beavers have been raising a garden on a vacant lot for several years. We start the seeds in boxes in our houses, and then we transplant them outdoors in the spring."

"What do you raise?" asked a Tenderfoot.

"Vegetables mostly—tomatoes, cabbage, corn, onions—things that stand up well against insects and blight and develop early and grow a long time. After they are planted, the fellows in the Patrol take turns cultivating and caring for them. Last year we supplied all the families in the Patrol with vegetables for most of the summer."

"And the government wants us to do it?" asked the Tenderfoot. "I vote this Patrol has a Liberty Garden this summer."

The rest of the Scouts voted Yes, too.

The Patrol Leader went on with his story.

Growing a Liberty garden

"My big brother was a Scout in this Patrol during the war, and he earned a General MacArthur Green Thumb Award."

"What for?" asked the Tenderfoot.

65

"Growing a Green Thumb Garden for home food production," replied the Patrol Leader. "The Patrol had a garden of over 400 square feet. He told me that over 100,-000 Scouts had Victory Gardens. Nearly 6,000 won MacArthur Medals, and over 12,000 got certificates. Lots of city Scouts worked on farms and some Scout Councils had 'work camps' to raise food."

"My father was a Scout in the first World War," said the Tenderfoot. "He said Scout gardeners had a slogan: 'Every Scout to Feed a Soldier.' Over one-third of the Scouts had War Gardens. The Department of Agriculture gave them awards."

All the Patrols in Troop 7 voted to have Liberty Gardens. It was hard work, but the Scouts shared the job and enjoyed it. They studied their Merit Badge pamphlets on Gardening and Agriculture. Their Merit Badge Counselor taught and helped them.

"It sure is wonderful to harvest these squashes," said the Tenderfoot, several months later, as he wiped his face hot from the September sun.

"Maybe you didn't know," said the Counselor, "that gardening is such a popular hobby that more people like it than like baseball. It's popular with Scouts, too. Over 100,000 Scouts have earned the Gardening Merit Badge. And thousands of others are working in their Liberty Gardens." See BOY SCOUTS OF AMERICA, CONSERVATION, MERIT BADGES.

Geological Survey Maps. Maps prepared by the U.S. Geological Survey, Department of Commerce. They are scale maps, which means that distance measured on the map represents the actual distance on the ground. Some are to a scale of 1:62,-500, which means that one inch on the map means 62,500 inches on level ground, or a little less than one inch to the mile. See MAPS.

Gilwell Training Center. The International Scout Training Center in England, founded by Lord Baden-Powell. Thousands of Scout leaders from all over the world have been trained there in the Wood Badge Course. In the United States the Wood Badge Course has been adapted to American conditions. Wood Badge courses are given also in Canada. See WOOD BADGE TRAINING.

Gliders. Planes without motors which are flown or pulled through the air as kites. Pilots can soar for hours and cover great distances by taking advantage of the up currents of warm air. In 1935 records were established by gliders in Germany of 38 hours and 45 minutes in the air, 313 miles airline distance, and an altitude of 14,190 feet. See AIR EXPLORER.

Gold Honor Medal. The highest award in Scouting, given to a Scout who risks his life to save someone else. There are more than a thousand Scouts who have

The highest award in Scouting

been able to save lives because they were brave and had learned what to do when an accident happened.

For instance, there was Edward, twelve

Scouts do a Good Turn at Christmas

years old, a Second Class Scout in Connecticut. He and Paul were skating on a pool when the ice cracked and Paul broke through into deep water. Edward saw the ice break and remembered the ice-rescue pictures in his *Handbook*. He rallied several other skaters to form a human chain, threw himself flat on the ice, and inched his way toward the struggling boy. The ice creaked and bent under him but did not break. At last Edward could reach Paul with a hockey stick. "Catch hold of the stick, Paul," he cried. Paul caught the stick, and slowly Edward worked his way backward, with the other skaters pulling behind him, until he was able to pull Paul to safety.

A brave boy who risked his life for his friend. But it took Scout training and know-how as well as courage to make the rescue.

The Gold Honor medal is awarded through the National Court of Honor.

Good Turn. A soft snow is falling. The roofs of the houses, the lawns, the sidewalks, and streets are covered with a white blanket. In the night the windows of the homes sparkle with bright, gay lights. It is Christmas Eve and everyone is merry.

On the other side of the little town there is one house that is almost dark. A weak light flickers from behind drawn blinds. Inside the front room are several small children. They are talking about Christmas and Santa Claus. They discuss roller skates, dolls, toy trains, and candy canes, and one boy is sure he will get that bicycle.

Their mother, tears in her eyes, is busy trying to scrape together enough for their supper. Christmas has come at an unfortunate time. The father is in the hospital; he has been there for a week. There is no money in the house even for food.

A knock comes at the door. The children

67

shout in glee, "Santa Claus!" They knew he would come. But on their mother's face there is a look of anxiety. She fears it will be more bad news.

The mother goes to the door. When she opens it she is greeted by a cheerful, smiling face. Behind are other cheerful, smiling faces.

"Merry Christmas!" says the boy at the door.

They are Scouts, in uniform, their arms loaded with bundles and bags of food, toys, and clothing. Not just several Scouts, but a whole Troop.

The Scouts had heard of this family's misfortune, and they had decided to make them happy on Christmas. This was their Good Turn.

This is a true story and it happened one Christmas Eve in New London, Connecticut. It illustrates the Scout Spirit in doing a Good Turn.

To the Scout a Good Turn—a Daily Good Turn—becomes a habit. It is one of the first things the Scout learns. Point Three of the Scout Law says, "A SCOUT IS HELPFUL." It says the Scout "must be prepared at any time to save a life, help injured persons, and share the home duties. He must do at least one Good Turn to someone every day."

Good Turns are little things and big things. A Good Turn might be just the answering of a question in giving a direction to someone. It might be helping an aged or blind person across the street. It might be the saving of a human life.

The Good Turn is *service*. It is giving or doing something for other people without expecting a reward or praise.

The Good Turn is *service* and *citizenship*. For service is closely connected with citizenship. Becoming a good citizen is the ambition of the Scout. So Good Turns lead to service and service to citizenship. See CITIZENSHIP, SCOUT OATH AND LAW.

Grand Howl. A ceremony of Cub Scouts used for opening or closing a meeting or for honoring a visitor. The Cubs form a circle and then all join in a long howl: "A-h-h-Kay-LA!" (Akela). The custom is taken from Kipling's *Jungle Stories,* where the wolf pack formed a circle and howled. See AKELA, CUB SCOUT, DEN.

Grasslands. Usually open stretches of land, free of large trees or shrubs, which are exposed to wind, rain, and sun and are covered with carpets of plants which grow close to the ground. A grassland, too, might consist of a front lawn, a back yard, or a meadow or pasture.

The Great Plains with their stretches of prairie are grasslands, and they played an

The Great Plains have stretches of grasslands

important part in the history of America. Once the buffalo and the Indian roamed them, and the fleetest animals, such as the deer and antelope, lived there. It was there the first great herds of cattle were raised, and across them went the exciting cattle drives of days not long ago.

Grasslands may not at first glimpse look exciting. Yet to the Scout grasslands offer excitement and adventure. There is probably not a foot of such land that does not contain something worth looking at and studying.

The Scout learns the importance of grasslands, not only as grazing grounds for cows, horses, and sheep but also as retainers of water. He learns, too, that grass and other growths help protect the soil and prevent erosion.

Grassland conservation is a popular Scout project. The Scout wants to help preserve America's soil. There is a Merit Badge dealing with grasses, legumes, and forage crops, as well as one for conservation. See CONSERVATION, MERIT BADGES.

Green Bar Patrol. Often called Green Bar Council. A Patrol may be made up entirely of Patrol Leaders who meet as a group monthly. The Scoutmaster is the leader of the Green Bar Patrol, and he trains the members of the Patrol to run their own Patrols effectively.

Patrol Leaders and Assistant Patrol Leaders are sometimes called "Green Bar Men," from the color of the bars they wear to indicate their office. See PATROL LEADER.

Ground Beds. The making of a comfortable ground bed is an important camping trick. The kind of ground bed to make depends on the country and the length of time the Scout is to remain in one place.

If he is traveling light and intends to stay but one night in a place, the Scout smooths off the ground, digs shallow shoulder and hip holes, and spreads out his waterproof ground cloth, with the bedding on top. The shoulder and hip holes are the comfort secret in sleeping on the ground.

Making a comfortable ground bed

When he is to remain two or three days in wooded country, the Scout collects a pile of dead leaves and wraps the ground cloth around them to form a mattress. If he is remaining for a week, he makes a frame of notched or staked logs and fills this with leaves. The ground cloth is spread over the leaves, with the bedding on top. See CAMPING (ADVENTURE), EXPLORER, SURVIVAL TECHNIQUES.

Grubmaster. A Scout who buys, stores, and distributes the food for the Patrol on hikes and in camp. He is in charge of cooking, and plans the menus for the Patrol meals. See PATROL.

Gun Safety and Shooting. See MARKSMAN'S CODE.

Handbook for Boys. The basic Scout handbook and first book published by the Boy Scouts of America. During the period since its publication in 1910, it has been the nation's best seller, next to the Bible, with a total sale of some 13,000,000 copies.

The *Handbook for Boys* helps boys to be good hikers and campers, and teaches the skills of Scouting, first aid, swimming, safety, nature adventuring, wildlife and woodlore, tracking and trailing, conservation and forestry, cooking, handicraft, and many other things. It guides Scouts along the trail of self-reliance, citizenship, and physical fitness. To those who are not in Scouting it is a handbook of ideals, practical information, and all sorts of outdoor skills.

The book represents the experience of many people—experts in Scouting and in technical matters. In the Preface of the 1952 edition are these lines:

"It is our hope that it will inspire you and help you to be watchful for opportunities to help other people, to be tolerant and respectful of the rights of others, to be courageous and self-reliant—in other words, to be a good American." See BOY SCOUTS OF AMERICA.

Handclasp. The Scout Handclasp is made with the left hand, the hand nearest the heart. When an American Scout meets a Scout from Canada or some other country, he uses the straight left-hand clasp.

Scouts have a special handclasp

In the United States, Scouts use the left hand with the three middle fingers in the same position as the Scout Sign. The little finger and thumb are spread apart and the fingers of each Scout are interlocked as their hands clasp. See SCOUT SIGN.

Handicrafts. Skilled types of work done with the hands for fun, usefulness, and profit. From Cub Scouting through

Exploring, boys and young men practice many kinds of handicrafts, some dealing with camp and some with the Merit Badge plan, such as tin-can craft, horncraft, basketry, leatherwork, woodwork, and metalwork.

Making a pack basket calls for skill

The Cub Scout likes to make things because it is fun. Cub Scouts make many articles useful around the house, such as tie racks, bookends, carpet beaters, and letter openers. They do beadwork and make Indian costumes.

The Boy Scout takes pride in making his own hiking and camping equipment and first aid kits. He can turn out a pair of snowshoes; make packs of various kinds, archery gear, and birdhouses; and build boats and canoes.

The Patrol as a whole also engages in handicraft projects. The Scouts repair Christmas toys to be given as a part of Christmas Good Turns and make things which can be sold to swell the Patrol budget. See HORN AND BONE CRAFT, MERIT BADGES, TIN-CAN AND WIRE CRAFTS.

Headdress, Indian. See INDIAN COSTUME.

Health. The state of feeling well, being physically strong and ready for anything. The day a boy enters Scouting he promises to keep himself ". . . *physically strong, mentally awake, and morally straight.*"

The Scout tries to get fit and stay fit. He tries to develop his body so that he has it under perfect control—supple, quick and easy of movement, and with a strong heart and lungs. Such a body helps to carry him through whatever he starts, and prepares him for more difficult things in later life. The Scout wants to know how to take care of himself.

Scouting activities lead to good health and physical fitness. Camping is a fine builder of a sturdy body. Hiking makes a Scout strong. Scout games are planned to build the body and make mind and muscles act in accord.

Getting a physical checkup

The Scout visits his family physician regularly each year for a physical checkup. He tries to correct remediable physical defects. He sees his dentist regularly, too, and learns how to brush his teeth and care for them.

He sleeps from ten to eleven hours, with his bedroom window open. He uses plenty of soap and water and bathes frequently. He learns how to care for his feet, especially on hikes.

The Scout is careful about his eating. He drinks a pint of milk each day. He has fresh fruit or fruit juices, meat or fish, green vegetables, butter and bread, and cereal each day. He eats and drinks slowly.

In preserving his health he learns personal first aid.

Knowing his body is in good shape gives him a feeling of self-confidence. The Scouts have a slogan: "Health through Knowledge, Safety through Skill." See FIRST AID, SCOUT OATH AND LAW.

Heliograph.   See SIGNALS.

Helpful, A Scout Is. The third point of the Scout Law suggests the way a Scout can help other people at all times. It reads: "A SCOUT IS HELPFUL. He must be prepared at any time to save life, help injured persons, and share the home duties. He must do at least one 'Good Turn' to someone every day." See "BE PREPARED," GOOD TURN, SCOUT OATH AND LAW.

Hikemaster. Member of a Patrol appointed by the Patrol Leader to locate the best places within a radius of several miles for every kind of hike and camping trip. The Hikemaster goes looking for these places himself and asks Scoutmasters and leaders of other Troops, so that he is always prepared to make good suggestions to his Patrol. See HIKES (KINDS OF), PATROL.

Hike (Second Class). One of the requirements for Second Class rank. With his Patrol, or with one approved companion, the Scout must take a hike, properly clothed and equipped.

A test hike for Second Class Scouts

On this hike the Scout must cover a total distance of not less than five miles, following a route indicated on a map or map sketch. He must show correct hike style and highway safety, cook a meal, clean up, and return from the hike in good condition.

The Second Class Hike is the climax of all the Second Class requirements. The Scout uses the skills he has learned, and when he has accomplished it successfully, he is a Scout Hiker. See SECOND CLASS SCOUT.

Hikes (Kinds of). There are hikes and hikes . . . and hikes. Hikes that are for a day, and hikes that last for weeks. Hikes for fun and hikes for adventure. Hiking is one of the most stimulating of Scouting activities.

Here are a few of the many kinds of hikes that Scouts take.

Adventure Hike. Scouts are sent out in buddy teams with instructions to look for adventure, then meet again at a certain place at a certain time to exchange experiences around a campfire.

Collecting Hike. A form of nature hike in which the Scouts bring back leaf prints, track casts, water life, or pressed flowers.

Conservation Hike. This includes tree planting, cutting of trails, erection of birdhouses, or putting up of feeding stations. Local game and forestry experts suggest activities and give leadership.

Exploration Hike. Scouts are taken into a strange territory. They may explore a mountain, cave, or lake, or set out to find the source of a small stream or river. This hike is full of surprises.

Good Turn Hike. Much like the Adventure Hike, but in this one the Scouts look for opportunities to do Good Turns. Their reports are written out, turned in without signatures, and read around the campfire.

Know-Your-Tree-Hike. This is a nature hike and is held in the fall or winter. Scouts identify trees, and often make a twig collection for school or the Troop meeting room.

North Pole Hike. A hike with toboggans or sleds in snow country. Two Patrols may race, Polar-exploration fashion, by following a map on which the Scoutmaster has marked a starting and a finishing point.

Orienteering Hike. With a topographic map and compass, Scouts are sent off in teams at five-minute intervals along a route where there are five or six landmarks. The Scouts who locate the landmarks are the orientation experts.

Robinson Crusoe (Survival) Hike. A hike in which the Scout takes cooking utensils but no food. He gathers wild plants, roots, berries, and fruits that are good to eat. For such a hike, he first must have had some nature study to know what plants in his section are edible.

Tracking Hike. A form of hike which is more exciting when there is snow on the ground. The Scouts follow the tracks of various animals. If there is no snow, other Scouts are sent ahead with tracking irons

or a whifflepoof to make a trail for the rest of the Patrol to follow.

Then there are Treasure Hikes, Signal Hikes, Flapjack Hikes, Historical Hikes, Father-and-Son Hikes, Ten-Mile Hikes, and many others. There is a Merit Badge for advanced hikers. See Bird Hiking, Conservation, Father-and-Son Hike, Flowering Plants, Maps, Survival Techniques, Whifflepoof.

A North Pole Hike is really rugged

Hiking Techniques. The Scouts in the Patrol were strung out, walking along silently. They had been talking and laughing a half hour before. Now they were all silent. There was plenty to talk about, too. They were in a beautiful rolling country. Now and then a rabbit ran across their trail just ahead. Birds were singing in the trees.

The Patrol Leader, up ahead, suddenly noticed that everyone was silent. Then he remembered what an old-timer had told him:

"Whenever there is no talk or singing, you know the pace is too fast."

The Patrol Leader realized the group had been making extra-good time. He slowed down and passed the word along. After five minutes the Scouts, now going along at an easy pace, were laughing and talking. Some were singing.

There is an art to hiking. There are some simple rules to be followed to make it more fun for Scouts. One of these rules is not to walk too fast on a long hike. Resting for short periods is better than walking a long distance and resting for a long time. While hiking, the Scout is careful about eating. If he eats too much, he becomes "logy" and wants to rest some more.

Knowing how to walk is important. The Scout learns to walk Indian fashion and not with his toes turned out. Surprising as it may seem, if one walks with his toes turned out he loses five hundred steps in five miles of hiking!

On level ground the Scout walks so that his foot comes down lightly on the heel and his toes reach forward to get a grip. This gives an even up-and-down motion. The type of ground he is covering has much to do with his way of walking. He walks with the least effort possible.

Feet should receive careful attention. Toenails are trimmed square across, the feet are covered with clean socks and shod with comfortable shoes, with thick soles. New shoes always are broken in before a hike. Tender places and blisters are covered with thin gauze, held on with adhesive tape.

Hiking techniques include many other things. Proper clothing, the proper kind of pack for a long or short hike, waterproofing matches by dipping them in melted paraffin or coating them with nail polish, first aid kits, good maps, knowing how to read maps, means of purifying drinking water, safety on trail or highway, and knowing what to do when lost—these are all things important to hiking. See First Aid Kits, Hikes (Kinds of), Merit Badges, Packs (For Carrying), Songs.

Hitches. A hitch is a knot that fastens a rope to another object such as a log or post. It may be used to fasten two ropes together if one of the ropes is stationary. There are

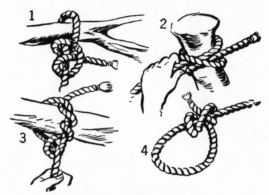

1. Two half hitches 2. Clove hitch
3. Timber hitch   4. Tautline hitch

many kinds of hitches, such as the half-hitch, clove hitch, tautline hitch, and timber hitch. Hitches are the basis of many other knots. See Knots, Lashings, Splices.

Hobbies. Activities in which a Scout takes a deep interest and at which he likes to work. Hobbies may be collections, handicrafts, or some sort of recreation like fishing. Sometimes hobbies become full-time, paying occupations, and other times they are just leisure-time pleasures.

Among the Merit Badge projects are many subjects that Scouts have developed into lifelong hobbies and sometimes a life work. Such activities as archery, art, bookbinding, coin collecting, gardening, nut culture, photography, pigeon raising, pottery, stamp collecting, and taxidermy give lifelong pleasure and profit. Others, such as forestry, printing, plumbing, and salesmanship, may lead to a career. See Collections, Merit Badges.

74

"Come and get it!" The Troop halts for a campfire meal

Holdfast. A mechanical device which can be gripped to a rope to secure it and hold it in place. There are many types of holdfasts, and these include all kinds of gadgets, snap hooks, and fastenings. One of the most important holdfasts in Scouting is the piece of wood used as a tension adjustment on tent ropes. See TENTS.

Home Duties. One of the first promises a Scout makes is to share the home duties. This is in the third point of the Scout Law, which says "A SCOUT IS HELPFUL." The Scout considers duties around the house or farm a part of his regular job and cheerfully performs such duties. See HOME REPAIRS, HOUSEHOLD SAFETY, SCOUT OATH AND LAW.

Home Repairs. Mother calls out that she simply cannot tie a knot in the clothesline so that it will hold. Her son, a Scout,

A Scout is helpful around the house

runs out, ties the right kind of knot, and the clothesline is there to stay. This is one of the many things a Scout can do around his home.

The Scout is an expert repair man. He is especially interested in home repairs as a

Merit Badge requirement. He can fix an electric plug or lamp socket; he can replace a faucet washer; he can hang curtains and repair curtain rods. He can even mend clothing and socks, or install a radio or television aerial. He is handy around the house. See HOME DUTIES, HOUSEHOLD SAFETY, MERIT BADGES.

Hornaday Award. This is an award for outstanding service to conservation. It is one which Scouts, Explorers, and Scouters prize highly. The award is given by the New York Zoological Society in honor of its first director, William T. Hornaday, who devoted his life to the cause of conservation and the preservation of wildlife. Dr. Hornaday in 1906 helped found the American Bison Society to save the American bison from extinction. He was an author, lecturer, and organizer in the interest of birds and mammals.

The Hornaday Award is also given to Troops which carry through a constructive program of conservation projects. See BALANCE OF NATURE, CONSERVATION.

Horn and Bone Craft. Many attractive and useful things can be made from horn and bone. This craft is especially popular with Scouts in rural districts, where the materials are plentiful, although Scouts in the city make fine horn handicraft, too.

Horn is more easily worked than bone. When boiled, it can be flattened and bent into shapes which it retains when cool. It also can be welded when heated. Bone and horn can be worked with ordinary files, knives, and drills. The Scouts make neckerchief slides, buckles, buttons, and many other things from both horn and bone.

With a cowhorn from which the bone has been removed, a "Robin Hood hunting horn" can be made. The tip of the

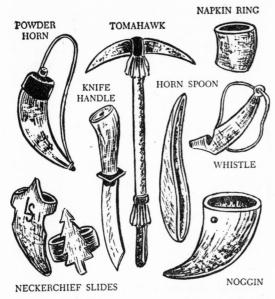

POWDER
HORN

TOMAHAWK

NAPKIN RING

KNIFE
HANDLE

HORN SPOON

WHISTLE

NECKERCHIEF SLIDES

NOGGIN

Horn and bone articles made by Scouts

Horseback Expedition. One of the first Explorer Posts ever organized was mounted. Each one of its members owned or could ride a horse. It is one of the most wonderful ways of exploring. There are also mounted Troops of Scouts.

Horseback expeditions are one of the most popular activities at Philmont Scout Ranch. There are 230 saddle horses making up six horse strings used by campers. Over 320 burros serve as pack animals. The best horse for expeditions is a good cow pony which is at home on the prairie or in the mountains and is sturdy and sure-footed. See Camping (Adventure), Explorer, Philmont Scout Ranch.

horn is sawed off. With a ⅜-inch drill a hole is then bored through into the large hollow section of the horn. A hollow brass tube is placed in this hole, and into the brass tube is inserted a brass reed. The reed may be securely fastened inside the brass tubing by turning down the tubing slightly and applying cement, then inserting the reed. Such a horn gives a rich, mellow tone. See Handicrafts.

Household Safety. The Scout is prepared to protect his home in an emergency. He knows how to get in touch with a doctor or hospital, how to report a fire, and how to call the police or sheriff. His first aid skill is useful in the home, too, for more accidents happen in the home than anywhere else. He learns about safety and accident hazards and helps to prevent accidents. He is a useful member of the household. See Fires and Firemanship, Safety through Skill.

Ice Rescue. Even the thickest ice is sometimes dangerous. So-called "air holes" are caused by strong currents or springs. In the spring the sun and rain weaken the ice so that it gives way easily.

Quick action counts in ice rescue

When rescuing someone who has fallen through the ice, the first thing a Scout does is to call loudly for help, and keep on calling. But meantime he slides a pole, fence rail, sled, or board toward the person in the water. The victim holds onto the pole, and the Scout, lying flat, pulls him out.

Should the Scout himself fall through, and there is no one to aid him, he supports himself with one hand on the ice and breaks off the thin edges of the ice until he has reached strong ice. He then slides his arms over the edge, kicks his feet up and down, and forces himself up and forward. When out of the water, he rolls sideways from the hole to spread his weight over a large surface. See FIRST AID.

Imu. "Let's have an imu!" exclaims one of the Scouts while preparing for a camping trip. That settles it, for everyone considers imu one of the most tasty meals prepared in camp.

A hole eighteen inches deep and eighteen inches square is dug and lined with rocks. A pile of crisscross firewood is built up on a platform of split wood. On the third layer of wood is placed a layer of flat stones. The fire is kept blazing until the stones are almost white-hot. Stones and coals are then leveled off in the bottom of the hole.

Vegetable tops or sweet leaves—wild grape, sweet gum, sycamore—are moistened and thrown in. On top of the leaves is placed a two-and-one-half-pound chicken or game bird for every three Scouts. And for each Scout there is one white potato, one sweet potato, one carrot, two ears of corn, one green banana, and, for dessert, one apple. All this is covered with more leaves, then a piece of dampened heavy canvas or burlap, and all is buried beneath earth so that no steam can escape. In three to four hours it is time to feast. See Cooking without Utensils, Fire Building.

Indian Costume. The clothing or costume of the American Indian consisted mainly of skins, feathers, and paint. The Indian obtained everything he needed right from nature and, being a great hunter, he killed his game with the idea of obtaining not only food, but clothing, tools, and utensils as well. The things the Indian wore and made were well adapted to his mode of life.

The Scout has profited in many ways from the red man's wisdom and nature lore. The Scout learns about Indians that once roamed the land in which he lives. For Indian ceremonies, the Scout often makes an Indian costume complete and correct, consisting of headdress, shirt, leggings or kilt, and moccasins.

The Scout employs materials as like as possible to those used by Indians. The Indian used the hides of the deer, buffalo, bear, caribou, and other animals. He made robes from woven skins of smaller animals. He made decorations from the quills of the porcupine, and beads from shells, bones, claws, teeth, and even berries. He used the coarse hair of animals for braiding and decoration. Feathers of birds were made into robes, dresses, and headdresses.

Moccasins protected and covered the Indian's feet. The Timber Indians had a soft-soled moccasin made entirely in one piece, sewed to a tongue or flap at the top. The Plains Indians had a moccasin made in two pieces, one of rawhide for the

sole and the other of soft buckskin for the upper. The moccasins were gaily decorated.

Indians loved bright colors. In many cases colors and designs on their clothes, or on their faces and bodies, had a meaning. There were colors for a man and colors for a woman, for the four points of the compass, and for war and peace.

Scouts make complete Indian costumes

Men wore moccasins, breech clout, leggings, and robe. Women wrapped around themselves a wide piece of skin or woven material for a dress, and sometimes wore a jacket. The Sioux and many western tribes wore the drooping feather headdress. Some wore only one or two feathers, but all such feathers had a meaning.

Because of the picturesque dress of the Dakota Indians, made popular by Buffalo Bill Cody in his Wild West Show, this dress has become recognized as an official costume of the American Indian. Even paintings of the Pilgrim Fathers show the red men dressed as Dakotas. A Seminole Indian marching in the Presidential Inaugural Parade at Washington might be dressed as a Dakota Sioux chief. Poca-

79

hontas was once painted in the dress of a Sioux bride.

The Scout is familiar with the different costumes of different tribes, and in making his outfit he uses materials which do not necessitate the wanton destruction of animals. See BEADWORK, INDIAN HANDICRAFT, MOCCASINS.

Indian Handicraft. *Peck! . . . Peck! . . . Peck!* The sound of one piece of stone striking another could be heard from the back yard. This sound had been going on all Saturday morning.

"What is Freddie building, a stone house?" finally asked his father.

"No, he's making some sort of Indian weapon," replied his mother.

"He must be hollowing out a stone canoe," decided Freddie's father. "I think I'll go out and take a look."

He went out the kitchen door into the back yard. Freddie was seated cross-legged beneath a shade tree, working away. The pecking sound continued.

An Indian tomahawk

"I thought maybe you were a stone mason building a new foundation for the garage," said Freddie's father as he came up. "Why are you sitting there knocking two small pieces of rock together? What are you doing?"

"I'm making an Indian stone tomahawk, Dad," explained Freddie.

"But you've been pecking away all morning. Let me see what you have done."

Freddie handed his father a piece of stone, pointed on one end and thick on the other. Around the thick part was the beginning of a small groove. He had been making this groove for the handle by chipping at the stone with another round piece of stone.

"Say, that's beginning to look like a real tomahawk!" exclaimed his father. "But you seem to be doing it the hard way. I've got a lot of tools in the basement. What do you say we go down there and get a couple of files and work on this? Maybe the emery wheel could do a better job."

"No, Dad," said Freddie firmly. "That's not the point. I'm making this the way Indians made it. They used this batter stone —this round stone—to batter and peck away the groove. The idea is not just getting the groove in the stone, but getting it there as the Indians did."

"I see," mused his father. "But this is going to take a long, long time, isn't it?"

"Sure, but I'll be proud when I get it done as the Indians did it—with just another stone."

"I believe you have something there," answered his father. "I think this is a great project. It shows that you have not only patience but determination. And, as you say, doing a thing as the Indians did it will give you a lot of satisfaction."

Freddie's father was an understanding father. He became interested right away. During his youth he had not been a Scout and now he saw what he had missed. He suggested that after supper he and Freddie go over to the public library and look up some of the annual reports of the Bureau of American Ethnology, which describe many of the primitive ways in which Indians did things.

Making things "Indian fashion" interested Freddie so much that he wanted to

Indian moccasins and tom-tom

earn the Indian Lore Merit Badge. He and his Patrol buddies were making all kinds of Indian things—headdresses, breech clouts, leggings, tom-toms, weapons, and moccasins, and decorating them in Indian fashion. They flaked arrowheads and made bows. Soon the Patrol was the best-dressed band of "Indians" in the Troop. See ARROWHEADS, BEADWORK, INDIAN COSTUME, MERIT BADGES, MOCCASINS.

Scouts learn Indian signs

Indian Sign Language. A language of signs and gestures by which different tribes of Plains Indians talked with one another. Indians did not have an alphabet and could not spell out words, but made signs for things and ideas only.

One of the requirements for the Indian Lore Merit Badge is a knowledge of Indian sign language. Like the Indian, the Scout learns to use one or both hands. For instance, he points to the position in the sky where the sun would be at a certain time. Sign language is as simple as that. To indicate a full day the Scout points to the east and moves his finger over his head to the west.

Scouts are required to learn at least fifty signs in the Indian sign language as part of the Merit Badge requirements. See MERIT BADGES.

Insects. Living in this world are countless numbers of marvelous little creatures. Insects are the original Mighty Midgets. If a boy were as strong, as agile, and as swift in proportion to his size as an insect, he could win every event in the Olympic Games singlehanded.

Scouts study and make collections of insects. They learn which kinds live in the desert, the forest, the grasslands, and the marshes. They learn how the mosquito finds you in the dark, how a bee keeps on the "bee-beam" in flying home, why insects sleep with their eyes open, why a daddy longlegs is not an insect. They learn about the life histories of insects in their collections. Many Scouts earn the Insect Life Merit Badge for their special projects in studying insects. See BALANCE OF NATURE, COLLECTIONS, CONSERVATION, DESERT LIVING, FORESTS, GRASSLANDS, MARSHES, MERIT BADGES, SURVIVAL TECHNIQUES.

Insignia. See BADGES AND INSIGNIA.

International Conference. A conference of the leaders in World Scouting held every two years to maintain high standards of Scouting and exchange methods and techniques. Each of the fifty-two Scout Associations has six delegates to the Conference. See INTERNATIONAL SCOUT BUREAU, JAMBOREE (WORLD), WORLD SCOUTING.

International Flag Code. A method of signaling with flags which is understood by seafaring peoples of all nations. The rules are set forth in the *International Code Book*. See SEA EXPLORER.

International Morse Code. A system whereby dots and dashes are used to represent letters and numerals in signaling. The Morse Code was developed by Samuel Finley Breese Morse (1791-1872), an American artist and inventor, who originated the magnetic telegraph.

The International Morse Code, which is slightly different from the American Morse Code, is standard throughout the world. The Scout employs it not only in wireless and electric-buzzer messages, but in flag signaling (wigwagging), smoke signaling, and in many other ways. See SIGNALS.

International Scout Bureau. Headquarters of the International Scout Conference in London, England. It is supported by the fifty-two Scout Associations. Col. John Skinner Wilson is Secretary. Correspondence and questions on World Scout-

ing clear through the International Scout Bureau.

Interpreter. A Scout at World Jamborees who serves as guide and interpreter to Scouts from other countries. He wears a special Interpreter's Badge to show the language in which he is an expert.

Investiture Ceremonies. Ceremonies at which a candidate becomes a Tenderfoot Scout, or new Troops are installed in Scouting.

At the Investiture ceremony, the Tenderfoot Scout takes the Scout Oath in the presence of the Troop. As the Scoutmaster gives the badge to the new Scout, he says something like this: "Candidate, I have given you a Badge which has been worn with honor and distinction by Scouts who have gone before you. This shows our friendship for you and the trust we place in you. By the authority vested in me by the National Council, Boy Scouts of America, I make you a Tenderfoot Scout."

Unit Investiture ceremonies are more elaborate, and often include parents, members of the church or other group which sponsors the Unit, and friends. See CAMPFIRE CEREMONIES, CEREMONIES, COURT OF HONOR.

Jamboree (National). A big national camping event which brings together Scouts from every state in the Union. A Jamboree is a great demonstration of camping skills and pageantry. It gives Scouts a chance to form new friendships and learn how other fellows do Scouting.

The first National Jamboree was held in Washington, D.C., in 1937 at the invitation of the President. At this event 27,232 Scouts and Leaders took part in the big camp at the foot of Washington Monument. In July of 1950 the Boy Scouts of America climaxed its fortieth anniversary celebration with the second National Jamboree at Valley Forge, Pennsylvania. A National Jamboree normally is held every four years, and during the months before each event Scouts are busily engaged in "jamboneering," a term meaning to make their own equipment. Such equipment includes tenting, packs, bedding, charcoal burners, Patrol and kitchen supply boxes, Patrol flags and Patrol totems. See JAMBOREE (WORLD).

Jamboree (World). When a boy becomes a Scout, he joins a great world-wide brotherhood. Every four years thousands of Scouts from the fifty-two Scout Associations meet in one big camp at a World Jamboree.

Here they have two weeks of fellowship, showing one another their favorite Scouting skills and how they camp back home. There are demonstrations of Scouting, large pageants showing history and national costumes and customs, with flags flying and bands playing songs of many lands. Scouts who cannot speak the same language live as friends together and talk by signs and gestures in a queer language of their own called "jamboreze," made up of words and expressions from different languages. They swap articles with one another.

The first World Jamboree was held in England in 1920. At that time 301 Scouts from thirty-two countries attended. Other Jamborees have been held in Denmark (1924); England (1929); Hungary (1933); Holland (1937); France (1947). The seventh World Jamboree was held in Austria, 1951. When Baden-Powell, founder of Scouting, was asked why this event was called a Jamboree, he replied, "Can you think of a better word?" See JAMBOREE (NATIONAL), SWAPPIN'.

Scouts from many lands meet at a World Jamboree

James E. West Conservation Scholarship. A scholarship awarded by the Ladies Auxiliary to the Veterans of Foreign Wars in memory of the great Chief Scout. It is presented to a Scout who has done outstanding work in conservation, and the money is to be used for future study of conservation practices and skills in college.

John Boat. A type of flat-bottom, square-end rowboat. Also called a "Mississippi John boat," "bateau," "Jo boat," or "punt." Scouts in the Middle West sometimes put up a tent at one end of a John boat and cruise down the river, pulling in to shore for the night. They spend the day fishing, swimming, and watching the river life as the boat drifts along down the river.

Judging. Skill in judging or measuring distances is a Scout requirement. Here is a method of judging distance where the Scout uses the visor of his winter cap or a broad-brimmed hat.

The Scout pulls his hat down over his eyes. He can see just beneath the brim. He stands rigid on the bank of the river and looks at a spot on the other side. This spot can just be seen beneath his hat brim. He sights at this point, which is level with the place where he stands.

He then turns, without lowering or raising his head, and looks from beneath his hat brim to see what object on this side of the river is in line with his eyes and his hat brim. Finding this to be the top of a small bush, he paces off the distance. In this way he finds the distance across the river.

This method is used by Scouts to judge or determine distances or widths on level ground. There are times when a Scout must be able to judge distance accurately without the use of instruments.

It may be in the case of a stream where he plans to build a bridge. Or one across which he plans to swim. If he knows he can swim only one hundred yards, he wants to be sure the stream is not wider. Distances over water are harder to judge than those over land.

Or the Scout may be cutting down a tree and want to know its height to determine whether it will fall on his tent or shelter.

It is important also to know one's own measurements. For instance, to know the length of one's step, as well as the length of one's foot.

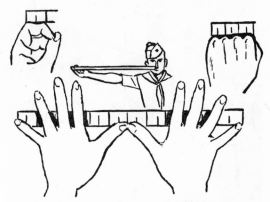

The Scout knows his own measurements

The Scout measures the span of his hand from thumb to little finger. He determines his reach with both arms extended to the side, the length being from the tips of the fingers on one hand to the tips of the fingers on the other. He measures the length of one arm extended, from the tip of the nose to the tip of the fingers. He reaches up and determines the distance from the tips of his fingers to the ground. All these personal measurements may come in handy in estimating or judging distance.

Many such measurements have been used in the past. The *brazada,* or length of the extended arms, is used in Mexico today, and a lariat is said to be so many *brazadas* in length. Some old-time store-keepers still measure cloth by estimating the yard from the chin to the tips of the fingers on one hand. In *Gulliver's Travels* the Lilliputians, when measuring Gulliver for a suit of clothes, used such measurements as "twice around the thumb is once around the wrist," and such short cuts. Artists figure a man's height in so many "heads."

Measuring height of a distant object

The "pencil method" of measuring is a favorite with Scouts. The pencil is held at arm's length with the thumb marking the point on the pencil corresponding with the base of the object to be measured. The arm must be level and the pencil straight up and down. The Scout now measures on the pencil some known height, the same distance away as the object to be measured.

He lays off this known distance upon the object the number of times required to reach the top. He adds these up and has the height of his object.

There are many other ways of finding distances and heights. They are to be found in the *Handbook for Boys*.

Besides distances and heights, the Scout learns to judge or estimate weights of objects. One way of testing this ability is to fill several sacks with different kinds of material. One may contain gravel, one sawdust, another grain of some kind, and another paper. Each member of the Patrol lifts each sack and tells how heavy he thinks it is.

Junior Assistant Scoutmaster. When an Explorer becomes sixteen years of age and is at least of First Class rank, he may be appointed Junior Assistant Scoutmaster upon recommendation of the Scoutmaster and the Troop Committee. The Junior Assistant may teach the Scouts of the Troop some subject in which he is expert, such as signaling or camping. Or he may serve as a leader if the Scoutmaster needs an additional leader for the Troop. The Junior Assistant Scoutmaster wears a badge of bronze and green. See SCOUTMASTER.

Junior Leaders' Training Conference. A special training event conducted for boy leaders of Troop or Explorer Units. These conferences are to help the Junior Leaders strengthen their leadership ability as well as their interest in Scouting. See LOCAL COUNCIL.

Kabob. A complete meal cooked on a stick. The stick, or a long metal skewer, is known as the *shish*, and among Oriental peoples the meal is called *shish kabob*.

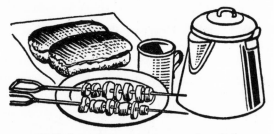

Kabob makes a tasty campfire dish

The first step is to make a spit from a green stick of some sweet wood, about as thick as a pencil. Sharpen one end. Cut one-quarter pound of meat into one-inch cubes. Cut an onion in half or in slices and remove the outer peel. Add potato and tomato slices. Skewer a piece of meat, then a piece of onion, then potato and tomato, then meat and onion, etc., until all is on the stick. Bacon may also be used. Broil close to hot coals, turning constantly. See Imu.

Keeper of the Buckskin. The member of a Cub Scout Den who acts as Scribe and keeps the Den records. See Den.

Kim's Game. This is a Scout game requiring a keen eye and a good memory. It is usually played by Patrols. The Scouts gather before a tray covered with a cloth. The cloth is lifted for a minute and the contestants are allowed to study the twenty or thirty small articles on the tray. Then they retire and make lists of the items they remember. The game is called "Kim's Game" from the character created by Kipling. See Games.

Kind, A Scout Is. Scouts are kind not only to pets and farm livestock, but to wild animals and birds. For birds which need special protection, they set up feeding stations and build birdhouses. Many Scouts construct wildlife refuges. The sixth point of the Scout Law says: "A scout is kind. He is a friend to animals. He will not kill nor hurt any living creature needlessly, but will strive to save and protect all harmless life." See Bird Feeders, Scout Oath and Law.

King's Scout. The highest rank in Scouting in Canada and Great Britain. The King's

Scout must be First Class, an Ambulance Man and either a Pathfinder or a Coast Watchman, and have two other badges from a required group. He is re-examined in all his badges annually.

The King's Scout Badge

Kit Carson Trek. A thrilling twelve-day high adventure trip through Philmont. Explorers carry their supplies in packs on their backs. They "top out" on five of the highest mountains, stopping overnight at Uracca Cow Camp, Miner's Park, Rincon Bonito, and Porcupine.

Knife. The Scout knife is one of the most useful articles the Scout carries. With it he can open a can of tomatoes, punch

The Scout knife has many uses

a hole in leather, loosen a screw, remove a bottle cap, or cut rope, as well as many other things.

In addition to the cutting blade the Scout knife has an awl, can opener, bottle opener, and screw driver which fold into the handle. The Scout's knife and belt axe are two valuable tools, and he protects them against bad usage and always keeps them sharp, dry, and clean. Here are some knife pointers that Scouts practice:

Keep your knife sharp and free from rust at all times.

For crude work, whittle AWAY from yourself to prevent injury. For advanced whittling, practice will teach you a variety of cuts.

When splitting a stick, do not hammer the back of the blade. It ruins the edge and weakens the hinge of a pocketknife.

Keep the blade away from fire. The heat draws the temper of the steel and makes it soft and useless.

When carrying your knife, keep a pocketknife closed, a sheath knife in its sheath.

Attach the sheath to the belt, back of the hip joint.

And finally: Don't play with your knife. A knife is a tool, not a toy!

Knots. "Save my child!" . . . The child is in grave danger, some thirty feet away from shore. The Scouts have only pieces of rope, not one of which is long enough to reach the drowning child.

But they work quickly and efficiently. One Scout ties his short rope with a sheet bend to the rope of the Scout next to him. The second Scout ties his rope with the same knot to the rope of the next boy. The rope becomes longer quicker than this paragraph can be read. The last Scout ties a bowline around himself and swims to the child. The others pull both back safely.

This is only a Scout game known as "Save My Child." The "child" sits on a burlap bag and the Scouts "rescue" him by showing their efficiency in knot tying.

But such accidents happen in real life. The Scout is prepared at all times to tie

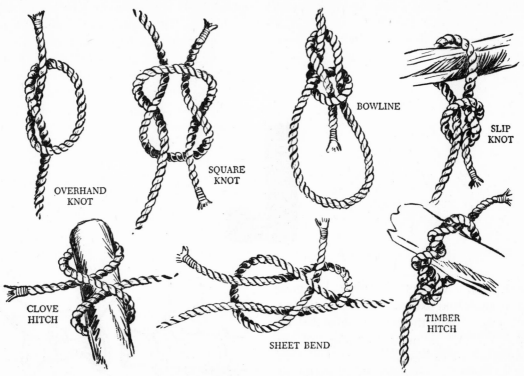

Types of simple and efficient knots the Scout learns to use

the right knot at the right time and at the right place. A knot in an emergency may be a matter of life or death.

Whether it is tying a package, making a lashing for the shear poles of a bridge, tying up a boat, or fastening the string to his bow, the Scout uses the proper knot.

The knots required for the Tenderfoot rank are those most generally used in camping and outdoor work. These are simple but highly efficient knots. They meet the tests of good knots, which are: (1) the knot fits the purpose for which it is needed; (2) it is easily tied; (3) it will hold until it is untied; and (4) it is as easily untied as tied and does not "jam."

The overhand knot is the simplest knot. Two overhand knots can form either a somewhat useless granny knot or a valuable square knot. It is all in the tying. The Scout uses the square knot with bights in tying his shoestrings. He uses the slip knot on his neckerchief and for other purposes.

The bowline knot has been called the "king of knots." It holds firmly when tied and is easily untied. There are various forms of bowlines, developed for different purposes.

Hitches are important. The clove hitch is a good knot for securing a boat's painter. The timber hitch is used for big and little jobs. The Scout uses it to fasten his bowstring to his bow.

There are a variety of bends and lashings. Bends are used to fasten one rope to another. Lashings are important in bridge work and many other projects.

Knots are so important in Scouting that at the bottom of the Scout Badge is portrayed a simple overhand knot—a reminder that a Scout does a Good Turn daily. It is a reminder, too, to "Be Prepared." See HITCHES, HOLDFAST, LASHINGS, ROPEWORK, TENDERFOOT SCOUT.

Lashings. A length of rope, his good sharp knife and axe, and plenty of timber, and what things the Scout can make! He needs no nails or metal fastenings of any kind. He uses lashings.

Lashings are rope or thong bindings used with poles or spars to make tripods and tables, bridges, signal towers, lean-tos, and many other important things around camp and in wilderness engineering.

In pioneer days, when there were no nails to be had in the forests or on the plains, almost every type of structure was put together with lashings. The cowboys built their corrals by lashing posts together with green rawhide which hardened like iron. The rafters and beams of the Mormon Temple at Salt Lake City are lashed together at the joints with *shaganappi,* or rawhide strings called also "Indian iron," and now after nearly a hundred years they still hold.

The Scout learns at least four important types of lashings. The most common is a *square lashing,* used wherever spars or poles are to be held together at right angles.

The *diagonal lashing* is employed to "spring" together two spars which do not touch where they cross. When the Scout

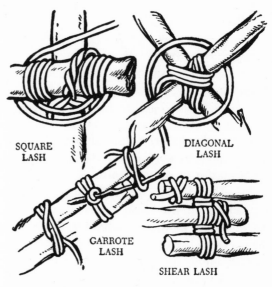

SQUARE LASH   DIAGONAL LASH

GARROTE LASH   SHEAR LASH

Lashings take the place of nails

wishes to lash together two parallel poles, he uses a *shear lashing.* If these poles are to be opened into shear legs, such as those used in making a Monkey Bridge, he makes the lashings slightly looser than usual and, when the spars are spread at the desired angle, the lashing tightens. Shear lashings also can be used by the Scout to bind three poles together so that they will open into a tripod.

For an extra-tight lashing a *garrote lash-*

ing is used. A "rack stick" is inserted under the knot and the rope twisted tight. The stick then is "seized" to the rope itself to holding the lashing secure. See BRIDGES, KNOTS.

Latrines. Sanitary latrines always are built a distance from the campsite and downhill from the water supply. When breaking camp, Scouts fill in the latrine and mound the dirt on top.

Law of the Pack. Four ideas for the Cub Scouts to follow every day. When he uses these ideas, he obeys the Law of the Pack. These ideas are: "The Cub Scout follows Akela; the Cub Scout helps the Pack go; the Pack helps the Cub Scout grow; the Cub Scout gives good will." See AKELA, CUB SCOUT.

Leaders. Every Scouting Unit has leaders. The Patrol Leader leads the Patrol, and there are other boy leaders in the Patrol with different responsibilities. The Troop has Troop leaders. The key boy leader is the Senior Patrol Leader, selected for this high honor because he is of First Class rank, a good leader, and a fine Scout. Another boy leader is the Junior Assistant Scoutmaster, an expert in some activity like signaling or first aid.

The Scoutmaster is the man who leads the Troop, and what a friend he is! He teaches the boys Scoutcraft and new games and brings them new adventures. He has one or more Assistant Scoutmasters.

The Troop Committee are Troop leaders too, often fathers of the Scouts in the Troop. Then there are Merit Badge Counselors, a fine group of men who coach Scouts in Merit Badge subjects.

In Cub Scouting there is a boy leader in the Den—the Denner—and a Boy Scout who is the Den Chief, and the Den

Mother. The Cubmaster and his Assistants and the Pack Committee are Pack leaders.

In Exploring, the Crew leaders lead the Crews, and the Explorer Advisor and Assistants lead the Unit. There are also committees with chairmen and other Unit officers.

Scouting helps boys develop into good leaders by giving them a chance to practice leading. See CUBMASTER, EXPLORER ADVISOR, PATROL LEADER, SCOUTMASTER, SENIOR PATROL LEADER.

Lifeboat Drill. A drill by Sea Explorers in which the crew demonstrates its ability to lower and man a lifeboat, as well as handle it in deep water under oars and auxiliary sail. See SEA EXPLORER.

Life Guard. See SCOUT LIFE GUARD.

A Scout saves a comrade's life

Life Saving. There was a terrific rumpus in Michael's room. It sounded as if four or five boys were roughhousing and things were being thrown about. Mother and Dad rushed from the living room to see what was happening.

When they opened Michael's door, a

strange sight met their eyes. Michael was standing in his shorts, breathing hard and looking triumphantly at his watch.

"Almost did it!" he cried.

"Did what?" demanded Dad.

"I almost got undressed in fifteen seconds. I did it in eighteen—"

"Why in the world do you want to get undressed in fifteen seconds?" asked his mother.

"A fellow doesn't jump in the water and rescue someone when he has all his clothes on," explained Michael. "He's got to get his clothes off—and quick! Fifteen seconds should be about the right time, my Scoutmaster says. He told us the way to practice was to see how fast we could undress when going to bed. To time ourselves. Get it down pat until we can shell out in fifteen flat. And I almost did it!"

His mother and father looked at each other and smiled. Already they could see their boy throwing off his clothes, jumping into the water, and rescuing a comrade. They were proud.

Scouts have long been noted for their work in saving lives. Since Scouting started in America, some 2,400 Scouts have received awards from the National Court of Honor for saving lives at the risk of their own. Some rescues involved other kinds of accidents, but most of them were drowning.

There are many other cases, too, unrecorded. Scouts have saved lives and never said a word about it. None but the Scouts themselves knew anything about it. Boasting is a quality not characteristic of Scouts.

Now many Scout methods of life saving and rescue work have been perfected, and because Scouts are trained, because they are prepared, they are able to save lives with less risk to themselves and others. See ARTIFICIAL RESPIRATION, "BE PREPARED," CARRIES, FIRST AID, GOLD HONOR MEDAL, GOOD TURN, ICE RESCUE.

Life Scout. The fifth rank in Scouting. For the Life Scout Award the Scout must have a satisfactory record as a Star Scout for a period of at least three months and must qualify for ten Merit Badges, some of which are in required subjects. Most important of all, he must meet requirements in Scout Spirit and Scout Participation. See MERIT BADGES, STAR SCOUT.

Lincoln Trail Hike. A historical hike to Lincoln's home and tomb in Springfield, Illinois, usually planned for Lincoln's Birthday, February 12. See HIKES (KINDS OF).

Lion. The fourth rank in Cub Scouting. When a boy is ten he may meet the requirements and be a Lion Cub Scout. See CUB SCOUT.

Living Circle. A Den ceremony which symbolizes that all Cub Scouts are friends. Each Cub Scout in the circle holds out his left hand into the circle with the palm down

The Living Circle symbolizes friendship

and the thumb pointing to the right. Each holds the thumb of the boy on his left, thus forming a circle. The right hand of each is held up in the Cub Scout Sign.

Local Council. The Local Scout Council is responsible for the Scouting in its area. It receives a charter from the National Council to conduct the program of Scouting. There is a Council Office, which handles the membership and advancement records of Scouts, and is the headquarters. The Local Council is made up of Scout districts. There are more than 540 Local Councils covering the entire United States and Territories. The Council organizes Camporees, training courses for Scoutmasters, summer camps, and many other events for districts and Troops. See CAMPING (LONG TERM), CAMPOREE.

Log. A record kept by various Scout Units. The log is usually compiled by the Scribe. The Patrol log is an up-to-date, vivid account of every Patrol activity. The Troop log contains the history and traditions of the Troop. A guest log is a record of speakers, entertainers, and visitors who sign the log. Explorers keep expedition or trail logs which are records of Explorer expeditions as well as guides to future expeditions. See CAMP LOG, SCRIBE.

Log Jockey. A Scout who rides logs in the water.

Log Rolling. Two Scouts stand on a log in the water, and try to make the log roll over while keeping their balance. The one who does not fall in, wins.

Lone Scout. A boy who lives in a section where there are no other boys of his own age to join with him in Scouting can become a Lone Scout. He does the same interesting things as other Scouts, and has a man known as a Lone Scout Friend and Counselor for his leader. There are Lone Cub Scouts and Lone Explorers too. Lone Scouts can form a Tribe and meet as a group at intervals. See BOY SCOUT, RURAL SCOUTING.

Lost! One good woodsman had this rule: "I'm not lost—it's my camp that's lost." Being completely befuddled about one's whereabouts is not a disgrace. But not being able to find one's way back to camp is strange, from the Scout's viewpoint.

A lost Scout signals for aid

The first rule is not to get lost. The second is to be prepared in case one becomes lost. The Scout carries a knife, compass, and waterproof matches. He makes mental note of landmarks which will help orient him.

But in case he is lost, he does not become panicky. If he has crossed a stream, highway, or railroad, he knows these will lead him to some settlement. He builds a bright fire at night and a smoky one during the day. If night comes when he is lost, he makes camp and does not wander in the dark. See DISTRESS SIGNALS.

Lost Person Search. "A child is lost!" There are few Scout Councils that have not heard these words with the plea that Scouts help in the search. Because Scouts are supposed to be prepared for anything and everything, parents and even police often turn to them for aid.

In a special pamphlet, "Lost," prepared

Scouts rescue a lost child after an all-night search

by the Boy Scouts of America, the method of organizing a Lost Person Search is given. This includes: (1) obtain a complete description, plus all facts that bear upon disappearance; (2) organize search crews, with trained men if possible, and appoint leaders; (3) decide and announce equipment, rations, and signals to be used; and (4) decide when and where to search, use maps, and employ search methods to fit the terrain.

But mainly, "Be prepared; train now for the search you may be called to make later." See LOST!

Loyal, A Scout Is. Loyalty starts at home. The Scout, in the second point of his Scout Law, promises to be loyal to his parents, the members of his Patrol and Troop, and to his country. This important point of the Law reads: "A SCOUT IS LOYAL. He is loyal to all to whom loyalty is due, his Scout leader, his home, and parents and country." See SCOUT OATH AND LAW.

Mammals. When you go to a zoo to see the animals, you will find birds, fishes, reptiles, and mammals. The warm-blooded creatures which nurse their young are known as mammals. These include bears, coyotes, deer, raccoons, mink, chipmunks, mice, and some of the fishlike aquatic animals such a whales. Man is a mammal. Scouts, in their activities, learn about mammals and how they live.

Sea Explorers practice a rescue drill

Man Overboard Drill. A rescue drill practiced by Sea Explorers. At the cry, "Man overboard!" everyone on the ship goes into action. Those near life rings heave them over the side to the man in the water. Engines are stopped. Men off watch climb the rigging, keeping their eyes on the man in the water and reporting his location. The crew on watch man the lifeboat. Others rig a tackle to hoist the man on board. A doctor stands by, and the cook heats water and warms blankets. See SEA EXPLORER.

Maps. Miles away, somewhere over the hill, was the camping place. It had been a long hike and the Scouts did not want to go any farther out of their way than necessary. It was mid-afternoon and they were anxious to make camp before dusk.

A halt was called. The Patrol Leader drew out a map, a U.S. Geological Survey Map, which had a scale of about one inch to the mile. In other words, an inch on the map meant almost a mile on the ground.

The Patrol Leader laid his map on the ground and on it placed his compass.

"We will first get the map true to the world," he said. The compass needle pointed to the magnetic north. The Patrol Leader moved the map about until the arrow marked MN (magnetic north) on the map pointed the same way as the compass needle.

Map reading is important in Scouting

"That series of crisscross lines there means a cemetery," continued the Leader, putting his finger on a symbol on the map.

"There it is over there," eagerly pointed out one of the Scouts.

"Right! Now let me see—"

The Leader marked the place on the map where the group was at the time. Then he measured off a distance to a symbol which meant a railroad track went through a cut. He began to figure on the edge of the map.

"It's just one and one-half inches to that railroad track," he said. "An inch on this map is 62,500 inches on the ground, or about a mile. That means the track is 7,812 feet from us or, with 5,280 feet to the mile, just about a mile and a half due west."

"I'll pace off the distance," offered one of the Scouts. "My step is two and one-half feet. When I've walked 3,125 steps, we will be at our camping place."

The boys started due west and soon came to the railroad in the cut. Then they took their directions again and long before dusk they were making camp.

Map reading, as well as map making or mapping out a territory, is important in Scouting. The Scout, with his map and compass, and knowing the distance of his own step, is never at a loss to know which way to travel or how far he must go.

In making their own maps Scouts find directions with their compasses and measure distances by stepping them off. Such a map may be made of a campsite or of a hike and is used for future reference. See COMPASS, JUDGING.

Mariner's Compass. See COMPASS.

Marksman's Code. The Scout Marksman's Code, which every Scout observes, is as follows:

1. A Scout treats every gun as a loaded gun, even though he has personally unloaded it.

2. A Scout points the muzzle of a gun in a safe direction when picking it up and laying it down.

A Scout handles a gun with care

3. A Scout opens the action of a gun immediately and makes sure it is not loaded.

4. A Scout opens the action of a gun before he passes it to another person.

5. A Scout never points a gun, loaded or unloaded, toy or real, at any human being under any circumstances.

6. A Scout strives to preserve harmless animals and birds, and does not wantonly shoot or kill merely for the sake of killing.

Mountain climbing is a rugged sport for Explorers

7. A Scout takes every precaution for the safety of others before shooting in the open.

8. A Scout cares for a firearm before he lays it aside.

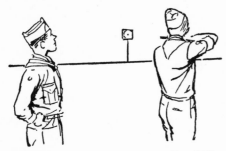

A Scout practices to acquire skill

9. A Scout is sportsmanlike when engaged in contests of skill with firearms and whenever handling firearms.

10. A Scout pledges never to shoot at anything he cannot positively identify.

11. A Scout knows and complies with the laws governing the use of firearms in his community and state. See CONSERVATION, MOSKEETO SHOOTING, SCOUT OATH AND LAW.

Marshes. The farmer leaned over the gate as he talked to the three boys. There was a twinkle in his eye. "So you want to play around in that old marsh of mine?" he asked.

The boys, Scouts, chorused enthusiastically: "Yes, sir!"

"But I can't see what you want to go down there for," went on the farmer. "My neighbors can't understand why I don't drain off that swamp—"

"Oh, no!" cried the Scouts in unison.

"Well, don't worry, boys. I won't do that. I remember, when I was a boy, I got a lot of fun wandering around and exploring that marsh. And now it is more interesting than ever. It has become a refuge, a sanctuary for many animals and birds—

they come here and they know they are safe. And right over there, where you see those cattails, you might find a muskrat. And over there a flock of ducks came in this morning—"

But with loud thanks the Scouts were off. They knew that marshes and bogs are living museums. To go bog-trotting is one of the most adventurous trips a Scout can take.

Bogs are islands of wildlife. Here are to be found rare plants like the fringed orchid, and interesting animals like the marsh wren. Some Scouts make collections of different peats in marshes. Peat is partially carbonized vegetable matter and is used in some countries as fuel. Certain plants can be found which show green leaves at the top while the bottoms are dead and beginning to form into peat.

Many interesting facts have been discovered about marshes and swamplands in recent years. Much of this type of land has been brought under cultivation and has

Marshes are wildlife refuges

been found to be the most productive on earth. However, it has been found that it would be a mistake to drain all such land. It is a necessary breeding place for ducks, and it offers food and shelter for birds and mammals useful to man. See CONSERVATION.

Measuring. See JUDGING.

Medal of Merit. An award made by the National Court of Honor to Scouts who perform an outstanding act of service, putting into practice Scout skill, but not necessarily involving a risk of life. Certificates of Merit also may be awarded for meritorious action. See NATIONAL COURT OF HONOR.

Merit Badge Counselor. An experienced man who is an expert in the field of a Merit Badge activity. He gives his time and skill in helping Scouts in his field and advising, coaching, and examining them on their projects. See MERIT BADGES.

Merit Badges. Many grown men who once were Scouts have felt that their entire lives were influenced by the Merit Badge Program. At an early age it opened up to them the work in which they were most interested, and they followed it through to become doctors, radio engineers, forest rangers, or scientific farmers, or to engage in many other worth-while careers. To others Merit Badge work has provided lifelong hobbies of fascinating interest.

By the time a boy is old enough to be a Second Class Scout he finds he likes to do certain things better than others. He may want to construct a radio set, make a model plane, or engage in first aid work rather than collect stamps, raise pigeons, or play football.

Through the Scout Merit Badge Plan the Scout is given (1) more skill in the things he likes to do, and (2) a chance to try out new activities so that he can find new things he likes. In the Merit Badge list there are 103 activities, each with its own instructive pamphlet. Here is the complete list:

MERIT BADGE GROUPS
1. *Campcraft:* Camping, Surveying, Pioneering, Cooking.
2. *Outdoor Sports:* Hiking, Fishing, Archery, Marksmanship, Cycling, Horsemanship, Skiing, Athletics.
3. *Aquatics:* Swimming, Rowing, Canoeing, Life Saving.
4. *Nature:* Nature, Astronomy, Bird Study, Botany, Insect Life, Reptile Study, Zoology, Weather.
5. *Conservation:* Soil and Water Conservation, Forestry, Wildlife Management.
6. *Personal Development:* Personal Fitness, Scholarship, Reading, Public Speaking, Business, Salesmanship, Farm Records and Bookkeeping.
7. *Citizenship:* Citizenship in the Home, Citizenship in the Community, Citizenship in the Nation, World Brotherhood.
8. *Public Service:* First Aid, Public Health, Safety, Fingerprinting, Firemanship.
9. *Animal Husbandry:* First Aid to Animals, Dog Care, Poultry Keeping, Pigeon Raising, Beekeeping, Beef Production, Hog and Pork Production, Sheep Farming, Animal Industry, Rabbit Raising, Dairying.
10. *Plant Cultivation:* Gardening, Landscape Gardening, Fruit Culture, Citrus Fruit Culture, Nut Culture, Agriculture, Corn Farming, Small Grains and Cereal Foods, Cotton Farming, Grasses, Legumes and Forage Crops.
11. *Communication:* Signaling, Bugling, Radio, Journalism, Printing.
12. *Transportation:* Automobiling, Aviation, Railroading, Seamanship.
13. *Building:* Farm Home and Its Planning, Farm Layout and Building Arrangement, Home Repairs, Machinery, Farm Mechanics, Wood-

Agriculture

Animal Industry

Archery

Architecture

Art

Astronomy

Athletics

Automobiling

Aviation

Basketry

Beef Production

Beekeeping

Bird Study

Bookbinding

Botany

Bugling

Business

Camping

Canoeing

Chemistry

Citizenship in the Community

Citizenship in the Home

Citizenship in the Nation

Citrus Fruit Culture

Coin Collecting

Cooking

Corn Farming

Cotton Farming

Cycling

Dairying

Dog Care

Dramatics

Electricity

Farm Home & Its Planning

Farm Layout & Bldg. Arrangement

Farm Mechanics

Farm Records & Bookkeeping

Finger-Printing

Firemanship

First Aid

First Aid to Animals

Fishing

Forestry

Fruit Culture

Gardening

Grasses, Legumes, & Forage Crops

Hiking

Hog and Pork Production

Home Repairs

Horsemanship

Indian Lore

Insect Life

Journalism

Landscape Gardening

Leatherwork

Life Saving

Scouts can earn Merit Badges in 103 different activities (SEE ALSO NEXT PAGE) work, Metalwork, Masonry, Painting, Plumbing, Electricity, Chemistry.

14. *Arts:* Art, Architecture, Mechanical Drawing, Photography, Sculpture, Woodcarving, Pottery, Music, Dramatics, Indian Lore.

15. *Crafts and Collections:* Basketry, Textiles, Bookbinding, Leatherwork, Coin Collecting, Stamp Collecting, Rocks and Minerals, Taxidermy.

See EAGLE SCOUT, FIRST CLASS SCOUT, LIFE SCOUT, SECOND CLASS SCOUT, STAR SCOUT.

Machinery	Marksmanship	Masonry	Mechanical Drawing	Metalwork	Music	Nature
Nut Culture	Painting	Personal Fitness	Photography	Pigeon Raising	Pioneering	Plumbing
Pottery	Poultry Keeping	Printing	Public Health	Public Speaking	Rabbit Raising	Radio
Railroading	Reading	Reptile Study	Rocks & Minerals	Rowing	Safety	Salesmanship
Scholarship	Sculpture	Seamanship	Sheep Farming	Signaling	Skiing	Small Grains & Cereal Foods
Soil & Water Conservation	Stamp Collecting	Surveying	Swimming	Taxidermy	Textiles	Weather
Wildlife Management	Woodcarving	Woodwork	World Brotherhood	Zoology		

Mess Kit. A collection of eating gear carried in a small bag. The mess kit consists of the mess bag—carried in a handy place in the pack—containing a plate, soup bowl, knife, fork, spoon, and teaspoon. Scouts often make their own mess bags. See PACKS (FOR CARRYING).

Moccasins. Foot coverings of soft buckskin or other leather worn by the American Indians. There are two general types of moccasins: the soft-sole kind of the Timber Indians and the hard-sole kind used by Plains Indians.

Two patterns for making moccasins

When buckskin is not to be had, the Scout makes his moccasins from split cowhide or other soft, tanned leathers. The easiest type of moccasin to make is the one-piece moccasin of the Nez Percé Indians which has a seam from the great toe along the side to the heel. A small tongue and tie string complete this simple moccasin. See INDIAN COSTUME.

Model Building. Making models of bridges, signal towers, campfires, trail marks, camp furniture, log cabins, airplanes and boats, and many other things is a favorite project with Scouts. The models are built to scale, or in exact proportion to the originals.

Monkey Bridge. See BRIDGES.

Moskeeto Shooting. A method of teaching Scouts and others the proper way of handling and using shotguns by employing a .22-caliber gun. The gun, especially built with a smooth-bore barrel, uses a shell containing small pellets instead of a bullet.

There are three stages in Moskeeto shooting. The student first shoots at stationary targets on the ground at 33-feet distance. He then shoots at an elevated coffee can at 35-feet distance, moving his gun upward and firing when in line with the target. Finally, he shoots at flying targets at from 65 to 75 feet. See MARKSMAN'S CODE.

Mushrooms. These members of the fungi family are either delicious food or deadly poison. Scouts who are not thoroughly familiar with mushrooms do not take chances. See WILD FOODS.

Music. See BUGLING, SONGS.

National Anthem. The "Star-Spangled Banner," composed by Francis Scott Key on September 14, 1814, was officially made the national anthem of the United States on March 31, 1931. Scouts, in showing respect for the national anthem, if not in uniform, rise, face toward the music and stand at attention, holding their hats over their hearts. If in uniform they rise and stand at salute.

National Audubon Society. A society founded in honor of John James Audubon, the American naturalist. With a membership of some five thousand, the society has general charge of the forty-four Audubon bird sanctuaries in Louisiana, Maine, Massachusetts, Michigan, Florida, Virginia, North and South Carolina, and elsewhere. Scouts co-operate with the society in their bird-feeding and bird-counting activities. Headquarters of the National Audubon Society are at 1000 Fifth Avenue, New York 28, New York. See BIRD FEEDERS, CONSERVATION.

National Council. The governing body of the Boy Scouts of America, chartered by Congress to administer the Scout pro-

gram. The majority of the members are representatives of Local Councils. All are adult men citizens who are volunteers. See BOY SCOUTS OF AMERICA.

National Court of Honor. A group of distinguished men who have the responsibility of recommending to the Executive Board Awards for Life Saving, for Meritorious Action, and Scholarship Awards.

National Jamboree. See JAMBOREE, (NATIONAL).

National Parks Service. A Federal agency whose function is to set up and maintain National Parks and National Monuments, and to protect the trees, plants, birds, and mammals within the parks. The National Parks Service is located in Washington, D.C. See CONSERVATION, FORESTS.

Nature. The existing universe, with all the things it contains and their marvels, unusual occurrences, and laws. To the Scout, nature means the grasslands, marshes and bogs, deserts, mountains, and forests, and all their wildlife and growing things. Nature is the clouds, sky, land, and water. See BALANCE OF NATURE, DESERT LIVING, FORESTS, GRASSLANDS, MARSHES, SURVIVAL TECHNIQUES, WILD FOODS.

Nature Crafts. Collections of wood specimens, rock samples, insects, bird feathers, leaves, and casts of animal tracks and the building of birdhouses all form interesting handicraft projects for Scouts.

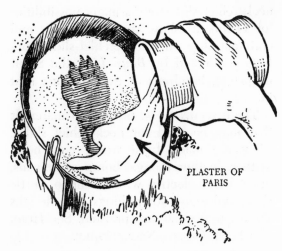

Making a cast of an animal track

While the Scout finds a nature museum a good means of learning about trees, shrubs, edible plants, and many types of birds, insects, and mammals in his own vicinity, he considers such a museum as a teaching aid only. He knows that nature must be learned out-of-doors at first hand from the live plants and animals in their own natural homes.

One of the most interesting of nature crafts, and an excellent example of this type of craftsmanship, is the taking of casts of leaves, twigs, and mammal and bird tracks. For this the Scout needs plaster of Paris, or modeling clay. Here is the procedure as explained in the official *Handbook for Patrol Leaders:*

"For leaf or twig casts, roll out a thin layer of modeling clay with a bottle. Lay the leaf on the clay, bottom-side down. Roll over the leaf with the bottle roller, until a good imprint is made. Remove the leaf. Build a one-inch wall of modeling clay around the imprint to form the mold. Pour dry plaster into a small amount of water, until the plaster begins to pile up in the middle in an 'island,' then stir thoroughly. The mixture should have the consistency of melted ice cream. Pour plaster into the form, then let it set for an hour or so. When hard, remove the modeling clay wall, and lift out the cast. Trim it with a knife, let it dry, then paint with ordinary water colors or with poster colors.

"Track casts are made directly from animal (mammal) or bird tracks found in the ground. Choose a good track. Place a ring around it, made from a one-inch strip of cardboard, fastened together with a pin or a clip. Pour plaster of Paris batter into the ring. Leave until the plaster is set. Wash the finished cast in running water to remove dirt." See BIRDHOUSES.

Marking a nature trail

Nature Trail. Basic training in nature adventuring or survival techniques starts on a nature trail. On such a trail Scouts come to recognize plants and animals in their natural environment.

The first step in making a nature trail is to find a location in a nearby natural area—desert, prairie, marsh, or forest—that has the largest number of typical common animals and plants. The trail need not be more than three or four hundred yards long and may be marked with simple markers such as painted stakes, brightly colored pieces of cardboard, or other devices that will mark the trail, and with signs identifying the plants and habitat of animals. See BALANCE OF NATURE, NATURE CRAFTS.

Navigation. A science which enables a seaman or airman to direct his ship or plane from place to place upon the sea or in the air and to determine his position at any time. The study of navigation is important to Sea Explorers and Air Explorers. See AIR EXPLORER, SEA EXPLORER, SHOOTING THE SUN.

A slide holds the neckerchief in place

Neckerchief. An important part of the uniform of Cub Scouts, Boy Scouts, and Sea Explorers. The neckerchief is folded smartly and snugly around the neck, with the insignia at the back, right side up and centered.

The neckerchief is secured by an official or a handmade neckerchief slide. Cub Scouts tie the ends of the neckerchief in a square knot. The Boy Scout ties the ends in a slip or overhand knot. Sea Explorers secure their neckerchiefs with a flat square knot instead of a slide, and the ends are not tied. Explorers and Air Explorers wear neckties. See BOY SCOUT, CUB SCOUT, EXPLORER, UNIFORMS.

Neckerchief Slide. The making of neckerchief slides offers many possibilities for Scouts to show their originality and craftsmanship. In neckerchief-slide contests conducted by *Boys' Life,* the Scout magazine, hundreds of examples are sent in.

There seems to be no end to materials that may be used for neckerchief slides. They are made from wood, cow horn, leather, leather thongs, bones of animals, birch bark, electric wire, bamboo, turtle shell, and many other things. The designs are often original and unusual. See HORN AND BONE CRAFT, NECKERCHIEF.

Neighborhood Commissioner. An experienced leader who aids the leaders of Troops, Packs, and Explorer Units in a given area. He is selected because of his thorough knowledge of Scouting. The work of the Neighborhood Commissioner is coordinated and supervised by the District Commissioner.

Neighborhood Patrol. A Patrol of two to eight country boys who live too far apart to form a Troop, who have a Scoutmaster and meet in each other's homes to have fun in Scouting. See RURAL SCOUTING.

Night Eyes. The Scout tries to learn how to use his eyes so that he can see in the dark. He knows that eyes have two different types of "seeing cells." One, in the center of the retina, is very sensitive to color and light and is used for daylight seeing. The other, found only on the edge of the retina, is color-blind and sees only in shades of gray or black.

It takes a half-hour in the dark before the night eyes begin to operate. Then vision comes, and the Scout knows that if he wishes to study some object he can see it better "out of the corner of his eye." In other words, he does not look at the object directly, but on one side.

Pioneers used noggin drinking cups

Noggin. A natural drinking cup made by hollowing out a tree burl, that knoblike growth created by nature in healing over wounds of broken-off branches. Pioneers, Indians, and frontiersmen carried noggins attached to their belts.

Sugar maple, ash, or hickory burls are best for making noggins. The green burl is more easily worked than the dead, dried-out ones. Often the green burl is found to be rotted inside, which aids in hollowing it out.

The grain in tree burls is usually curly and interwoven, so it is necessary to proceed slowly in the hollowing-out process. Indians sometimes used rounded stones, heated red hot, to burn out the center, cutting away charred portions after each burning; and they also employed a crooked knife. Scouts can work efficiently with ordinary wood-carving chisels.

The bark remains on the noggin until it is roughly hollowed out. Then the bark is removed and the inside is whittled smooth until the cup is about ⅜ inch thick. It is then sanded, greased thoroughly, and washed in hot water. A hole is burned or drilled in the end, and a thong with a toggle is tied on. The toggle slips beneath the Scout's belt.

In a showcase at Boy Scout headquarters in New York is a beautiful noggin of white-oak burl, owned by the late Dan Beard. In presenting it to the national organization "Uncle Dan" wrote:

"I have carried this noggin from the watershed of the Hudson Bay to the toenail of Florida, from Ocean Point, Maine, to the Olympic Mountains. Nobody but good fellows ever drank from this noggin." See BEARD.

Oath. See Scout Oath and Law.

Obedient, A Scout Is. Learning to take orders and carry them out cheerfully and promptly is a part of the Scout character. A good leader must first learn to obey. Scouts find that by obeying their leaders everyone has a good time in Scouting, and by obeying their parents they find their home life happy. The seventh point of the Scout Law reads: "A scout is obedient. He obeys his parents, Scoutmaster, Patrol Leader, and all duly constituted authorities." See Scout Oath and Law.

Order of the Arrow. A national brotherhood of Scout honor campers. Every Scout is eligible for membership in the Order of the Arrow, founded in 1915, if he proves his camping ability and Scouting knowledge.

Scouts are elected to this brotherhood by fellow-campers because they have shown ability in camping and because they have maintained a cheerful spirit in living up to the Scout Oath and Law in their daily lives, and because of their outstanding qualities of character and leadership and of service to others. Today there are Order of the Arrow lodges in 415 Councils, with a membership of 45,000. See Scout Oath and Law.

Orienteering. A compass game for almost any outdoor occasion, and one which may be played by either small or large groups. Orienteering has recently been made an Olympic Games sport. In Sweden and Norway it is as popular as football or baseball are here.

The course over which the game is

Orienteering is a compass game

played may be as small as 100 x 100 feet. Each player is given a score card, a pencil, and a compass. He starts at a marker which corresponds with the first "Starting Point" on his card. Players then "travel" according to the degrees and distances indicated on their cards. There are three starting points, and the player who reaches each destination correctly receives a score of 100. The highest possible score is 300, obtained when a player reaches all three destinations without error. See COMPASS, GAMES.

Ovens. There comes a time when the Scout will want to bake his own bread in camp. For this he will need an oven, and

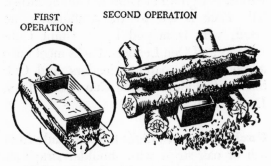

Making bread with an Ozark pan oven

he can make his own out of the simplest materials.

One type of oven is the *Ozark pan oven*. The dough is placed in a pan and heated on the bottom until it rises. Then the pan is placed between two burning logs, with two other burning logs across and on top.

The *reflector oven* is made from syrup or oil cans which are first cut in half diagonally. One half is used as the oven and the other half placed within the first and used as a shelf. This type of oven is placed beside the fire and not over it. See BISCUITS, DUTCH-OVEN COOKING.

"Overnight." Scout name for an overnight camping trip. The "Overnight" camp is a combination of hiking and camping. Patrols or Troops hike to a suitable campsite, set up shelters, cook their own meals, engage in various Scout activities, and after a night or two hike back home.

The "Overnight" is, first of all, practice in camping. Some Troops make as many as twenty-four "Overnights" a year. At such times the Scout has an opportunity to make use of the skills he has learned on hikes, to learn more about how to construct a comfortable camp, and to enjoy the pleasure of living with his comrades for a night or two. See CAMPING (LONG-TERM), CAMPOREE.

P-Q

Pacific Crest Trail. A mountain trail popular with Explorers and older Scouts. This majestic wilderness trail runs parallel to the Pacific coast from Canada to Mexico. Along its 2,265 miles are five National Parks and nineteen National Forests. From auto camps the Scout can backpack to Mount Rainier, Mount Hood, Glacier Peak, Mounts Shasta, Lassen, and Whitney, and explore California's Mission Land, Mexico, and Canada. See APPALACHIAN TRAIL.

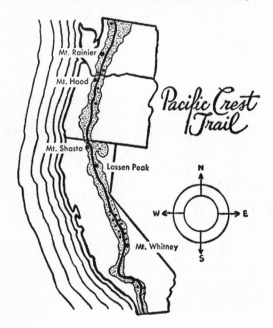

Pack. A group of Dens in Cub Scouting. The Pack is led by the Cubmaster, an adult, who is helped by Assistant Cubmasters and Den Leaders. Packs meet once a month with parents, leaders, and Cub Scouts. See CUBMASTER, CUB SCOUT, DEN, DEN MOTHER.

Pack Baskets. Light baskets made from ash or oak strips with shoulder straps attached. Being rigid they are good packs in which to carry breakable articles. Pack baskets are best for canoe trips. Scouts usually make their own pack baskets, following instructions shown in the Scout film, "Making a Pack Basket." See PACKS (FOR CARRYING).

Pack Frames. A packing harness designed for carrying awkward loads, such as duffel bags, or those which from their shape are uncomfortable to the back. When the pack frame is used, the pack itself is kept away from the carrier's back. The pack sits high so that the shoulders instead of the hips carry the load.

The pack frame is one of the oldest known forms of carrying harness. A number of kinds have been tried and tested

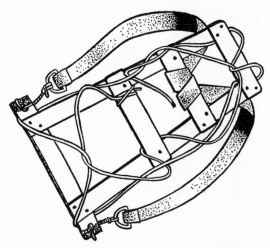

The pack frame helps carry heavy loads

for the use of Scouts. These include the Trapper Nelson and its modified version, the Trapper-O, the Dimond-O, and the more recent Form-Fitting type, developed by a Scouter. The latter type is fitted to each individual's back. See PACKS (FOR CARRYING).

Pack Leaders. These include members of the Pack Committee, a group of men who help the Cubmaster, usually fathers of the Cub Scouts in the Pack. The Den Dad is usually a member of this committee. The Pack Committee secures a meeting room, selects the Cubmaster and Assistants, and supervises finances. The church, school, or other group that operates the Pack selects the Pack Committee. See CUBMASTER, DEN DAD, DEN MOTHER.

Packs (For Carrying). There was once a fellow named Sindbad the Sailor. Sindbad in his travels happened upon another chap called the "Old Man of the Sea." The Old Man of the Sea got on Sindbad's back, and Sindbad could not get him off. This was one of the early types of packs which proved to be a lot of trouble and did not make the carrier happy.

Packs for carrying can be like the Old Man of the Sea on a fellow's back after he has hiked a few miles. Other packs can be a pleasure and comfort, and the Scout hardly notices that he is toting a load.

One thing that makes packs so interesting is that outdoorsmen never seem to be able to agree on just what is the best pack, as there is no one pack which can be used for all purposes. The Scout learns that the final test is the pack that suits him best.

It is also important to find a pack that will best suit all members of the Patrol. In this way the packs will be uniform, and the Patrol on a hike will present a smart appearance. Each pack carries the Patrol totem or emblem.

The many kinds of packs can be narrowed down to three general types. These are the *knapsack*, which is a large bag with shoulder straps; the *pack basket*, which is a basket with shoulder straps; and the *pack frame*, which is used for toting a bundle lashed to the frame.

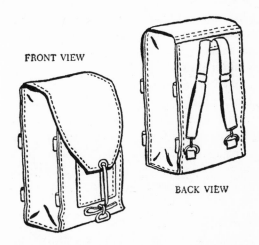

FRONT VIEW

BACK VIEW

A good pack is a pleasure and a comfort

The *Mohican pack* is considered a good all-around pack and is popular with Explorers. It has adjustable leather straps, and rings to which the axe, canteen,

109

poncho, and other small equipment may be attached on the outside of the pack itself. Scouts learn to make this pack, as they do most of their other packs and pack frames.

Pack baskets are comfortable but, being rigid, do not permit the Scout to stow a few things in them without having these things jostle around. However, it is easier to find things in them than to root around in a bag.

Pack frames, in the opinion of many woodsmen, are the ideal backpacking equipment. They can be made to fit the needs of almost any Scout.

The place for duffel bags is on the pack frame or pack harness. It is difficult to carry them otherwise, as they are clumsy and unwieldy. Sometimes the Scout uses a tumpline, Indian fashion, in carrying such a bag on a pack frame.

There are times when the Scout needs a pack and does not have one. Then he has to use his ingenuity in constructing one. He can convert a flour sack, feed sack, pillow case, or similar bag into a good pack. He can also tie up an extra pair of trousers and make a *pants pack*, using the legs as shoulder straps.

Another emergency pack is the *horse collar*, which can be made with a poncho, ground cloth, or blanket. All gear and equipment are rolled up in the poncho, for example, and carried in the shape of a horse collar on the back. See PACK BASKETS, PACK FRAMES, PONCHO, TUMPLINE.

Parbuckle. A method of lowering or raising a heavy round and long object, like a barrel or a log, without the aid of tackle. The middle of the rope is looped over a hook or post at the top of an incline and the ends are passed beneath and around, say, a barrel. By hauling on the ends of the rope with equal force the Scout can roll

Raising a log with a parbuckle

the barrel up the incline, and by slacking the rope he can ease it down. A plank to form an incline makes the job easier.

Parents' Night. A night when the parents of the Cub Scouts, Boy Scouts, or Explorers are invited to a dinner or a show to see what things the Scouts can do. It is an all-around friendly occasion and family get-together.

Participation, Scout. See SCOUT PARTICIPATION.

Patrol. The Patrol had been organized for a month. In it were four boys who had been brought up in the same neighborhood, gone to school together, and who had played together. In this gang all understood one another and had about the same interests.

There were three other boys in the Patrol, making seven in all, a good number for a Patrol. These boys went to a different school and had not belonged to the gang.

"I think it is a good idea to have them in our Patrol," explained Charles, one of the original four. "They will have some new ideas, and, well, they are a little different from us fellows in a lot of ways, and this will help our Patrol. It will be what the Scoutmaster calls more democratic, to have all kinds in our Patrol."

The others agreed. Charles, who was a First Class Scout, was elected Patrol Leader. The Patrol had a den and went on hikes and an overnight camping trip. But one thing was lacking.

"We've been going a month and we don't have a name," said Pete. That was it. They needed a name for the Patrol, and a totem, and a call.

They studied the *Handbook for Boys*, where names and calls and totems were suggested. But they did not want to take just any name that meant nothing special to the Patrol. They wanted something that fitted the Patrol.

Then one day one of the boys brought a buffalo robe to the den.

"Dad says we might find use for this rug," the boy explained. "He found it in the attic."

"I've got it!" exclaimed Charles. "We'll hang it on the wall. We'll call ourselves the Buffalo Patrol. How's that?"

"Great! Our totem will be the buffalo," said another.

"And our call will be 'Um-moowu,' as the buffalo goes."

"*Um-moowu!*" chorused the others.

The Scouts got busy. One designed a Patrol flag with a buffalo head on it. They used their emblem or totem on all their equipment and as a special Patrol signature.

A Patrol, which is a part of a Troop, is one of the smallest of democratic organizations. It elects its own leaders, and each member has something to say about the way the Patrol is run. It can include from two to eight boys, and six or eight has been found the best number.

Every Scout in a Patrol has a job. There is the Patrol Leader. Then the Assistant Patrol Leader. Also a Scribe, who keeps the records; a Patrol Treasurer, who col-

lects dues and keeps financial records; a Patrol Quartermaster, who is in charge of Patrol equipment; and possibly a Hikemaster, a Grubmaster, a Song and Cheer Leader, and maybe a Bugler. See PATROL CAMPING, PATROL LEADER, PATROL TOTEM, TROOP.

A Patrol talks things over

Patrol Camping. Camping by Patrols. A Troop camp is set up by Patrols, where each Patrol does its own cooking and the Scouts do things together under their own Patrol Leader. Sometimes an experienced Patrol may go camping alone.

The different types of Patrol camping include the *Overnight Camp,* which is a combination of hiking and camping; the *Camporee,* which is run on a Troop, District, or Council basis; the *Long-Term Camp,* which is camping in one spot for a week or more; and the *Traveling Camp,* which is a moving camp. See CAMPING (LONG-TERM), CAMPOREE, "OVERNIGHT," PATROL.

Patrol Leader. The Patrol Leader, as his name indicates, is the leader of a Patrol, the basic Scout Unit forming an intimate group of comrades and friends in a Troop.

This is a position of honor, inasmuch as the Leader is picked by the boys themselves, and it is one of the most important offices in Scouting.

The Patrol Leader says, "Come on!"

Usually the most experienced Scout in the group, the Patrol Leader leads his Patrol in Scoutcraft knowledge and in Scout Spirit. Usually he is a First Class Scout, or well on his way to becoming one, and he keeps in advance of the members of his Patrol and trains them in Scout skills, so that they, too, may go forward. He is familiar with their homes, their parents, and their schoolwork and is sympathetic and helpful.

The Patrol Leader is the one who points the way and makes every boy in the Patrol eager to do his part. He gets the whole gang working together in games, singing, Good Turns, and on hiking and camping trips. He sets an example for his Patrol by wearing his Scout uniform at all Scout activities and urges all his Scouts to do the same. His uniform is the same as the others—although, if he is over fourteen, he may wear the Explorer's uniform—and he is proud of the two green bars on his left sleeve, his badge of office.

The Patrol Leader is responsible for the regular business of his Patrol, the attendance, dues, and reports. He selects, or the Patrol selects, his Assistant Patrol Leader.

While responsible for the Patrol as a unit, the Patrol Leader assigns responsibility to each of his Scouts.

The Patrol Leader faithfully attends all sessions of the Troop Leaders' Council to receive training for his job and plan the program of the Troop. He also represents his Patrol at the Troop Leaders' Council, bringing before the Council the wishes of his Patrol and taking back to his Patrol the plans of the Council. He gets the Scouts of his Patrol to take part enthusiastically in all Troop activities.

The Patrol Leader is the sort of fellow who says "Come on," instead of "Go on," and this is the secret of his leadership ability and influence. He asks no one to do anything he would not do himself. He strives to make himself such a leader that each of the other Scouts in his Patrol will think, "I'll follow him, I guess, because he is the kind of fellow I would like to be myself." See PATROL, TROOP.

Patrol Totem. An emblem or design indicating the name of the Patrol, such as Eagle, Raccoon, or Buffalo. The Patrol uses it on its flag, on its Patrol medallion, on shirts, as a decoration for the Patrol den, and to mark all Patrol equipment. It is the Patrol "signature" and designates the name of the Patrol. See PATROL.

Paul Bunyan's Axemen. A club of Scouts and Leaders in the North Star

Council (Duluth, Minnesota) whose members become skilled in using and caring for their axes, and teach other Scouts their skills. Their badge is a double-bitted axe. Members must be at least fourteen years old and meet certain requirements of skill and safety rules.

Pencil Measuring. See JUDGING.

Personal First Aid. Giving first aid to oneself. The Scout learns how to dress small cuts and to take care of himself when injured and alone. If he feels faint, he lies down and raises his knees and feet. If he cuts an artery in his arm, he grasps the muscle of this arm just below the shoulder with the fingers of the other hand and with the thumb presses the artery hard against the bone until the bleeding stops. He can make a sling for a broken arm by holding the cloth with his teeth and working with his other hand. See FIRST AID.

Types of simple first aid bandages

Personal Measurements. See JUDGING.

Phillips, Waite. (1883——). Wealthy Oklahoma oil man who is best known to Scouts as the man who gave the magnificent Philmont Scout Ranch near Cimarron, New Mexico, to the Boy Scouts of America. Mr. Phillips also provided that income from the Philtower office building in Tulsa, Oklahoma, be used for the upkeep of the property. See PHILMONT SCOUT RANCH.

Philmont Scout Ranch. Philmont Scout Ranch, a gift to the Scouts by Waite Phillips, offers 127,000 acres of challenging adventure to Explorers. Each year thousands of them from all over the United States travel in groups to take part in unparalleled experiences. Philmont provides camping, experiences along mountain trails, trout fishing, horseback riding, and western sports. It develops the Explorer's Scouting skills and gives him rich knowledge to take to his Unit back home.

There are four primary base camps, six secondary base camps and fourteen trail camps. Two hundred and thirty saddle horses make up six horse strings used by the campers. Experiences include a four-day Cavalcade; a ten-day Kit Carson Hike; a twelve-day Exploring and Pioneering Hike; a thirteen-day Expedition; a twenty-three-day Wagon Train; a thirty-day Ranch Pioneering Trek; a Junior Leader Training Troop; and a Frontiersman Schedule.

An old gold mine has been reopened where Explorers can pan for gold. Wild game and birds abound. An eleven-and-a-half-foot mammoth tusk has been unearthed, and prehistoric marine deposits have been discovered.

Philmont is also a training center for Leaders, who come and bring their families for a wonderful outing.

Philtrek. A trek at Philmont for Leaders, corresponding to the Pioneering Trek for Explorers.

Photography. Hunting with a camera is one of the most enjoyable of Scout activities. The Scout can take pictures of

At Philmont, Scouts enjoy horseback riding and western sports

birds and mammals, plants, trails, and campsites. The photographs he takes of his companions on hikes and camping trips are among his treasures.

Photography is a Merit Badge subject. The Scout learns the parts of the camera and how to properly operate it. He can mix his own chemicals for developing and fixing. He finishes his own pictures. Knowledge of photography may lead to a life-long occupation. See MERIT BADGES.

Physical Fitness. See HEALTH.

Pioneer Trail Trek. This is a Philmont trek where Scouts carry all their equipment in packs and camp under pioneer conditions.

Pioneering. The Scout knows the skills which the American pioneer used when he pushed beyond the boundaries of civilization, braved the unbroken wilderness, and prepared the way for others. The Scout learns how to build a bridge without nails or spikes, how to make a shack, and how to lay a trail for others to follow without blazing or destroying trees.

He learns how to handle rope, and how to use it in building gateways and signal towers and to lash spars properly.

The Scout carries on the traditions of the old pioneer scouts. He knows how to take care of himself and others in the wilderness. He knows woods, fields, and marshes, what wild plants are good to eat, how to camp and cook and make himself comfortable under any conditions. See CAMPING (ADVENTURE), CONSERVATION, FORESTS, HIKING TECHNIQUES, MERIT BADGES, PIONEERS, SIGNALS.

Pioneers. Pioneers were rugged men who pushed westward to conquer a continent and open trails through the wilderness for the white settlers to follow. They wore buckskin clothes and coonskin caps. They were men of strong character, kind to the weak and unfortunate, and usually deeply religious. Johnny Appleseed, Daniel Boone, George Rogers Clark were typical pioneers in the early years of our country's history. From these the modern Scout gets his ideals of courage, service, and self-reliance.

After these pioneers came others, and just as there were eighteenth- and nineteenth-century pioneers, there also are twentieth-century pioneers in America. The pioneer always has been and always will be the leader in the front rank of man's fight for progress.

The pioneer lived a life of adventure

For by the term "pioneer" is meant one who prepares the way, who takes the lead in anything. It means one who goes on before to overcome the hardships and dangers and make it easier for others who follow. Among the modern pioneers we have the foresters, inventors, scientists and explorers, airmen and seamen.

Baden-Powell had this in mind when he defined Scouting. He said: "By the term Scouting is meant the work and attributes of backwoodsmen, explorers, hunters, seamen, airmen, pioneers, and frontiersmen."

So the word "pioneer" means, first of all, adventure for the Scout. This is as it should be. The pioneering type of adventure is the heritage of every American boy. It opens up to him the realm of wide spaces, woods, rivers, lakes, and mountains which are playgrounds where he will have this adventure and fun. It is the promise of camping life in the outdoors.

The Scout thrills at the tales of De Soto, La Salle, Robert Rogers, Daniel Boone, Lewis and Clark, Zebulon Pike, Père Marquette, Brigham Young, Kit Carson, David Crockett, General Frémont, and the thousands of fur traders, missionaries, ranchers, miners, pioneer farmers, government surveyors, pony-express riders, and frontier scouts and soldiers.

But he thrills, too, when he thinks of Admiral Byrd, the Wright Brothers, Audubon, Rear Admiral Peary, Amundsen, Wiley Post, and many, many others who have done their part in preparing the way so that others may safely follow. See BOONE, BRIDGER, CARSON, PIONEERING.

Plants, Edible. See WILD FOODS.

Plaster Casting. See NATURE CRAFTS.

Pledge of Allegiance. Every Scout pledges allegiance to the Flag of the United States, repeating the pledge authorized by Congress in June, 1942. This pledge is:

"I pledge allegiance to the Flag of the United States of America and to the Republic for which it stands, one nation indivisible, with liberty and justice for all." See FLAG CODE.

Poisonous Plants. There are three plants which often cause skin poisoning,

and the Scout learns to recognize them and avoid them. They are:

Poisonivy, which is recognized by the leaves which grow in separate groups of three. It is found in different places along the ground, over logs, up trees, or in shrubbery.

Poisonoak, which has leaves closely resembling those of the oak tree. It generally grows as a shrub or ground plant.

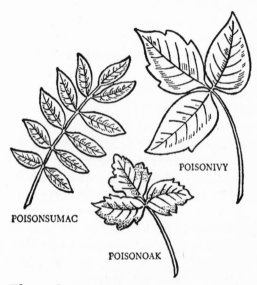

Three plants which cause skin poisoning

Poisonsumac, which resembles sumac, except that it has drooping clusters of white berries instead of the ordinary reddish sumac fruit. It is generally found in damp places.

Poncho. A waterproofed cloth with a hole in the center for the head to pass through. The poncho hangs over and protects the shoulders and body. Another type of poncho is made with a hood. Ponchos can serve many purposes on hikes and in camps. With his poncho a Scout can make a ground bed, an emergency shelter, or a ground cloth for his tent. See GROUND BEDS, PACKS (FOR CARRYING).

116

The waterproof poncho has many uses

Post, Explorer. See EXPLORER POST.

Powwow. A training conference for all Cub Pack leaders and prospective leaders, such as the Cubmaster, Den Mothers, and Pack Committeemen, new and experienced. It is held annually, and each Pack selects four people who are enrolled to represent their Pack in the four sections of the Powwow—games, handicraft, ceremonies and entertainment, and Pack administration. See CUB SCOUT, PACK.

Procedure Signs. Signs used in signaling when certain symbols of the Morse Code stand for words or expressions. Thus the word "Attention" is denoted by CQ on the radio or AA on the blinker. The word "Repeat" is sent as IMI on all signaling devices. The complete set of procedure signs is given in the *Handbook for Boys*. See SIGNALS.

Program-planning Committees. Committees which originate and recommend Explorer, Air Explorer, and Sea Explorer activities. Every Explorer Crew is represented on every committee and every Explorer is on at least one of the committees, so that everyone has a chance to help plan activities. There are four committees: Outdoor Committee, Social Committee, Service Committee, and Indoor Committee. See EXPLORER.

Public Health. If a mosquito bites you while his hind legs are in the air, watch out! This is the dangerous anopheles mosquito, a species that can transmit malaria. Other less-harmful mosquitoes usually bite with their hind legs on the surface of a person's skin.

Such knowledge concerns public health. It is important for the Scout and other young people to know a good deal about public health, because this subject tells how, by working together in villages, cities, counties, and states, authorities may hope to avoid the terrible losses and suffering which come from preventable diseases, such as typhoid fever, diphtheria, and malaria. Public health is a Merit Badge subject, but all Scouts learn and practice good public health procedures in their camps and at home. See MERIT BADGES.

Quarterdeck. A name applied to the aft part of the upper deck of a vessel, reserved for officers.

Quartermaster. A Troop or Patrol officer who looks after the equipment as well as Troop headquarters and the Patrol den. See PATROL, TROOP.

Quartermaster (Sea Explorer). The highest rank in Sea Exploring. See SEA EXPLORER.

Queen's Day. The Explorer writes the following letter to his mother: "Dear Mother: You are cordially invited to attend our QUEENS' DAY CEREMONIES next Tuesday night in Explorers' Hall. It will give me great pleasure to present you as my Queen and to wait on you in Court. (*Signed*) Your Devoted Slave." That is Mother's invitation to a ceremony in her honor. The "Royal Banquet" is prepared by the fathers!

Radio. The Scout was tapping out the "Q" signal—"QRA . . . QRA" ("What is the name of your station?") on his sending set. Finally there came through a faint response. He quickly consulted his log and found he was communicating with a station in South Africa! Not only that, but it was a radio "ham" who was a Scout he had met at the last World Jamboree!

The radio "ham," or amateur, is one who is well along in radio communication. He holds an amateur radio-station operator's license. But in the Scout program, there are opportunities to learn all phases of radio work. The Cub Scout learns to make and operate a crystal receiver as well as a receiver with one or more tubes. The Scout can earn a Merit Badge in radio. Radio sending and receiving are necessary to both Sea and Air Explorers and can lead into a lifelong profession. See INTERNATIONAL MORSE CODE, MERIT BADGES, SIGNALS.

Rafts. A float of logs or planks fastened together is the "pioneer's boat." There are times when the Scout or Explorer finds it necessary to build such a float to cross a stream and possibly to save a life.

Scouts build and use rafts

The most common form of raft is the log raft. This is made from five six-foot logs about six inches in diameter, chosen from dry timber deposited along the shore. These logs are lashed together, and the raft is pushed through the water by use of a long pole.

Scouts also construct coracle rafts by forming a ring of dry twigs lashed together and covered with a waterproof tarpaulin. By filling pup tents with dry sticks, rolling them into bundles, and lashing them together, the Scout can make a raft similar to the log raft. See EXPLORER.

Reading. See BOOKS.

Realistic First Aid. A first aid practice game in which accidents and injuries are imitated in so realistic a fashion that the fellow "not in the know" believes he has a real patient to work on. For example, in one course some Scouters heard a gunshot and, on investigating, found a hunter lying across a fence "bleeding" from a "bullet wound in his foot." They gave the "patient" the proper first aid at once just as if he had really been shot.

In a folder, "Using Experience Problems to Teach First Aid," prepared by the Health and Safety Service, Boy Scouts of America, instructions are given for "making up patients" so that they appear to be suffering from shock, fractures, snake bites, cuts, blisters, bullet wounds, and other illnesses and injuries. See ARTIFICIAL RESPIRATION; BONES, SPLINTS, AND GAUZE CARNIVAL; FIRST AID.

A Scout gives emergency first aid

Registration. All members of the Boy Scouts of America are registered. A boy is not a Scout and is not entitled to wear the uniform and badges of the Boy Scouts of America until he has been registered at the National Office. His membership starts after his registration is completed. See BOY SCOUTS OF AMERICA.

Religious Awards. To aid a Scout in fulfilling the religious ideals in his Scout Oath and Law, churches and synagogues of America have developed awards for Scouts of their faith. These are not Scout awards but may be worn on the Scout uniform, and they encourage the Scout to do his "duty to God." There are different requirements for each award.

There are five such awards: the Catholic "Ad Altare Dei"; the Jewish "Ner Tamid"; the Lutheran "Pro Deo et Patria"; the Protestant "God and Country"; the Mormon "Desert Recognition." See REVERENT, A SCOUT IS; SCOUT OATH AND LAW.

Reptiles. Cold-blooded, air-breathing, backboned creatures which are usually scaled, such as the snake, lizard, or crocodile. The Scout studies reptiles in the marshes, grasslands, prairies, rivers, and forests. He knows the poisonous types and how to treat their bites, and is also familiar with the harmless varieties. See BALANCE OF NATURE, CONSERVATION, DESERTS, FORESTS, GRASSLANDS, MARSHES.

Reverent, A Scout Is. In both the Scout Oath and the Scout Law his "duty to God" and his reverence toward God are emphasized. The Scout worships regularly with his family in his church or synagogue. He follows the religious teachings given him, is faithful in his church-school duties, and helps in church activities.

"Most great men in history have been men of deep religious faith," the *Handbook for Boys* tells. "Washington knelt in the snow to pray at Valley Forge. Lincoln always sought Divine guidance before each important decision. Be proud of your religious faith.

"Remember in doing your duty to God, to be grateful to Him. Whenever you succeed in doing something well, then thank

119

Reverence toward God is a part of Scout Law

Him for it. Sometimes when you look up into the starlit sky on a quiet night, and feel close to Him, thank Him as the Giver of all good things.

"One way to express your duty and your thankfulness to God is to help others, and this, too, is a part of your Scout promise."

The twelfth point of the Scout Law reads: "A SCOUT IS REVERENT. He is reverent toward God. He is faithful in his religious duties, and respects the convictions of others in matters of custom and religion."

This reverence means to the Scout the respect, regard, consideration, courtesy, devotion, and affection he has for some person, place, or thing that is holy. He shows his true reverence in two principal ways. First, he prays to God, he loves God, and he serves Him. Secondly, in his every-day actions he helps other people, because they are made by God in God's own likeness. The Scout and all others are important in the sight of God because God made them.

The Scout respects others whose religion and customs may differ from his own. He is not one of those who think it smart to tell stories or make fun of people of other religions or races. He knows that all his life he will be associating with people of other beliefs and customs, and considers it his duty to respect these people for their beliefs and customs, whatever they are.

This consideration is carried over into Scout activities. For instance, when such activities as Sunday hikes and camps are held, they are planned with the approval of parents and the clergy involved and are not allowed to interfere with the Scout's religious obligations.

Robinson Crusoe Hike. A "survival hike." The Scout takes his own cooking utensils but lives on nature. He gathers his foodstuff in the wild state. The Scout must be familiar with the local edible plants, roots, berries, and fruits. See SURVIVAL TECHNIQUES, WILD FOODS.

Roosevelt, Theodore (1858–1919). American statesman, editor, author, and twenty-sixth president of the United States. "Teddy" Roosevelt lived an active, exciting life. He led the Roughriders in the Spanish-American War, hunted big game in Africa, was a western rancher, and in 1914, on an expedition to Brazil, discovered a new river, *Rio Teodoro*.

Theodore Roosevelt was Honorary Vice-President of the Boy Scouts of America and Chief Scout Citizen. Each year a delegation of Scouts makes a pilgrimage to his grave at Oyster Bay, Long Island, New York. See BOY SCOUTS OF AMERICA.

Theodore Roosevelt—Chief Scout Citizen

Rope Spinning. The art of twirling or spinning a braided cord rope with the noose open. Rope spinning, perfected by cowboys, is a favorite sport with Scouts, especially at World Jamborees where the Scouts of different countries show the games and sports of their native lands.

A Scout demonstrates rope spinning

A special rope is needed in rope spinning, as ordinary rope or clothesline will not do. The rope spinner uses a braided cord rope, the best of which is "spot cord" Number 12. The rope is usually about twenty feet long. See ROPEWORK.

Ropework. The art of handling rope to a good purpose in tying knots and making lashings, hitches, bends, and splices. One of the sure ways of telling a real outdoorsman and camper is his knowledge of rope and its uses, and especially his ability to know the right knot to employ at the right time and to tie it quickly.

There are many kinds of rope, but for the Scout there are, generally speaking, but two kinds. One is the *laid rope*, which is important for pioneering and camping. The other is the *braided rope*, used for lifelines, spinning ropes, flagpole halyards, and for lashing on packs.

Rope has been defined as anything in cordage over one inch in circumference. Smaller cordage is twine or string. A hawser is a plain laid rope big enough for towing or mooring. A cable is three hawsers or ropes twisted and laid up.

Laid rope usually is made of manila (fiber of a banana-like plant), hemp, sisal, jute, or cotton fibers, first twisted into what are termed yarns. Two or more yarns are twisted into strands, and three or four strands are twisted and laid together to form the rope. It is the twist that holds the rope together, as yarns and strands are twisted against one another and the friction keeps them in place.

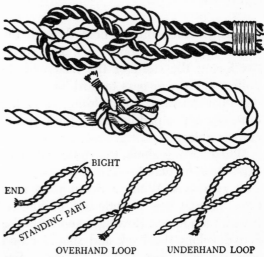

END   BIGHT   STANDING PART

OVERHAND LOOP   UNDERHAND LOOP

The outdoorsman is skilled in ropework

A braided rope, such as clothesline or sash cord, is made of strands of cotton or other material in a round braid. Braided rope is good for practice lariats, but cowboys use a three-strand manila or hemp rope for lariats.

In ropework the names of the parts of a rope are important. The "standing part" is that part of the rope not being worked at the time. The "end," or "working end," is the business end of the rope and the part that is being worked.

A *bight* is formed in a rope by turning the working end of the rope so that it lies along the standing part. A bight becomes a *loop* when the two parts of the rope cross—an *overhand loop* when the end is over the standing part, and an *underhand loop* when the end is underneath.

The simplest of knots is the *overhand knot*. This is made by first making an underhand or overhand loop and passing the working end around the standing part and through the loop. See HITCHES, KNOTS, LASHINGS, MERIT BADGES.

Rover Scout. An Explorer who is eighteen years old may be a Rover Scout. See EXPLORER.

Rowing. Propelling a boat through the water with one or more oars. The rower sits facing the stern of the boat and, in pulling the oar or oars toward him, forces the boat forward. In paddling it is the other way. The paddler faces the way the craft is going.

When rowing alone, the rower uses two oars. Or there may be several rowers, each with two oars. When a Scout rows in a crew, he may use a single oar, pulling on it with both hands. Rowing is good exercise and develops the back and shoulder and arm muscles. See BOATS (TYPES), SEA EXPLORER.

Rural Scouting. Scouting is open to every boy of Scout age in the nation, no matter if he lives in an area where there are no other boys of the required age to join with him. If a boy is a farm boy, or lives in a small village where there are not five boys (the least number necessary to form a Troop) of the proper age, he may join with one or two and form a Neighborhood Patrol with a man for Scoutmaster. In case there is not even one other boy of Scout age to join with him, he can become a Lone Scout. Lone Scouts can form a Tribe and meet now and then for Scouting and fun. See LONE SCOUT, NEIGHBORHOOD PATROL.

Rustic Furniture. Camp articles such as tables, chairs, benches, washstands, drying racks, and shelves made from deadtree limbs and stumps. Scouts employ con-

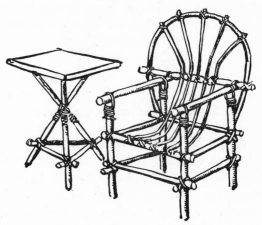

Scouts make rustic furniture

siderable ingenuity in making camp or rustic furniture. Poles are lashed together with rope or handmade twine and the natural shapes of logs and branches are utilized in constructing the furniture. See HANDICRAFTS, LASHINGS.

Safety through Skill. The Scout lives a life of adventure. He learns how to do things skillfully and so is able to do them safely. There are many things which are dangerous unless they are done well. If they are done skillfully, however, they can be done safely. Such activities are: swimming, canoeing, horseback riding, mountaineering, using an axe and knife, bicycling, and hiking. The Scout avoids risks which no amount of skill can make safe, such as walking across trestles, trying to beat trains over crossings, looking down gun barrels, playing with blasting caps.

His safety rule is "Safety through Skill"; skill not only in performance but also in *picking out and throwing out* the things where the odds are against him.

"Prevention" to the Scout is just another way of saying "Be Prepared." He prevents accidents before they have a chance to happen. He makes a safety inspection of his home, looking for inflammable rubbish, milk bottles on window sills, loose or worn electric fixtures.

He avoids foolish risks, and observes traffic rules. When hiking on the open road, he walks in single file, facing the traffic, and stays to the extreme left side of the road so he can see an approaching vehicle and the driver can see him. At night he displays a white cloth or handkerchief around his neck or right arm—preferably one in front and one in back. He carries a flashlight or lantern.

On the highway, Scouts follow safety rules

If he has a bicycle he practices the rules of bicycle safety.

He knows the rules of safety with firearms and how to use his axe and knife.

Scout camps require a medical examination from each Scout before he is admitted,

123

and train Scouts in the skills that enable them to take care of themselves and others in the open.

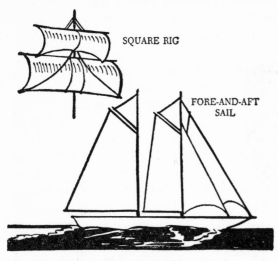

Types of sails

The Scout knows that the slogan "Safety through Skill" is the basis of a happy and adventurous life. See FIRST AID, HEALTH, HIKING.

Sail. A piece of canvas or other material attached to the masts or yards of a vessel in such a way that the wind blows it and thus moves the vessel along. There are many types of sail, the two general classes being the fore-and-aft sail and the square-rigged. The simplest of the fore-and-aft type boat is the catboat with its single sail. See BOATS (TYPES), SEA EXPLORER, SHIPS.

Schiff, John M. President of the Boy Scouts of America. Elected 1951.

Schiff, Mortimer L. One of the founders of the Boy Scouts of America, International Commissioner, and at the time of his death in 1931, the president.

Schiff Scout Reservation. Located at Mendham, New Jersey. It was given by the mother of Mortimer L. Schiff as a memorial to her son in 1932, and is now the home of the National Training Center. Scout leaders from all over the United States come to the Schiff Reservation for training.

Schuck, Arthur A. Chief Scout Executive. Appointed in 1948.

Scout Badge. The design of the Scout Badge is the sign of the north of the mariner's compass. This is the badge of the First Class rank. The miniature trefoil is the Universal Badge and, with minor changes, is used in all countries of the world as a sign of Scout Brotherhood, good citizenship, and friendliness.

The three points, like the three fingers of the Scout Sign, signify the three parts of the Scout Oath. The two stars symbolize the truth and knowledge which are the foundations of strong Scout citizenship. The

The First Class Scout Badge

eagle, national emblem of the United States, represents freedom and readiness to defend it. The scroll at the bottom of the badge turns upward like the corners of the Scout's mouth in a smile. On this scroll are the words of the Scout Motto, "Be Prepared." The knot, at the bottom, is to remind the Scout of the importance of the Daily Good Turn.

The Tenderfoot wears only the trefoil; the Second Class Scout only the scroll. The First Class Scout wears the trefoil and scroll combined. See CITIZENSHIP, FIRST CLASS SCOUT, SCOUT OATH AND LAW, SCOUT SIGN, SECOND CLASS SCOUT, TENDERFOOT SCOUT.

Scout Citizen. See CITIZENSHIP.

Scout Code. The rules in the game of Scouting. They include the Scout Oath or Promise and Law, the Scout Motto, and the Scout Slogan. See ATHENIAN OATH, CITIZENSHIP, SCOUT MOTTO, SCOUT OATH AND LAW, SCOUT SLOGAN.

Scoutcraft. A requirement for advancement in Scouting. By learning Scoutcraft the Scout becomes a good hiker and camper and outdoorsman, and a good citizen. See ADVANCEMENT, CITIZENSHIP, COURT OF HONOR, SCOUT PARTICIPATION, SCOUT SPIRIT.

Scouter. An adult registered member of the Scout organization who is eighteen years of age or over.

Scouter's Award and Scouter's Key. A Scouter's Award is a recognition for Scout leaders who, over a period of three years have met certain requirements in four fields: training, performance, service, and tenure in office. The Scouter's Key is an award for a Scoutmaster, Cubmaster, Explorer Advisor, or Commissioner who meets similar requirements.

Scout Executive. A full-time paid director of Scouting in a Local Council. He is aided by Assistant Scout Executives and Field and District Executives. See LOCAL COUNCIL.

Scouting for Physically Handicapped Boys. There are more than 250 Scouting Units made up of physically handicapped boys in hospitals and special schools for the physically handicapped. Included are those who are crippled, blind, deaf, cardiac, post-polio, cerebral palsied, and the chronically sick. There are also Scout Troops in colonies for those with Hansen's disease (leprosy) at Carville, Louisiana, and Molokai, Hawaii. Some Units have been in operation for twenty-five years or more. There are also hundreds of handicapped boys in normal Scout Units, carrying on the regular Scout program.

Scout Life Guard. A First Class Scout or Explorer who has met the twelve Scout Life Guard requirements. Such a Scout has the satisfaction of knowing that he has shown real ability and made a fine start toward becoming an outstanding waterman. He helps at the camp waterfront and is always ready to assist anyone who gets into difficulties in the water.

The requirements include being able to swim one-quarter of a mile in good form; having earned Swimming and Rowing Merit Badges, and either the Red Cross Junior or Senior Life Saving Certificate or the Life Saving Merit Badge. See LIFE SAVING, MERIT BADGES, SWIMMING.

Scoutmaster. A man volunteer leader of a Troop. The Scoutmaster is a key man in Scouting. He teaches games and Scoutcraft, and trains the boy leaders to run their own Patrols and the Troop. He encourages Scouts to advance in skill and is a friend and a hero to the Troop.

The Scoutmaster takes special training to learn new games and skills and outdoor

125

activities. He takes the Troop hiking and camping. He is helped by one or more Assistant Scoutmasters, who carry out the Scoutmaster's responsibilities if he cannot be there. See ASSISTANT SCOUTMASTER, TROOP.

The Scoutmaster is a friend and leader

Scout Motto. Part of the Scout Code. The Motto is "Be Prepared." It means the Scout is prepared at any moment to do his duty and to face danger, if necessary, to help others. In the Middle Ages the knights had a similar motto, "Be Always Ready." Someone once asked Baden-Powell, the founder of Scouting, "Be prepared for what?" "Oh," replied Baden-Powell, "for any old thing!" See "BE PREPARED," SCOUT CODE.

Scout Oath and Law. Johnny was busy mowing the front lawn on a hot summer afternoon when one of his Scout friends came along and stopped to talk to him.

"Hi," he called.

"Hi, Bobby," replied Johnny.

"How about coming along with me to the movies? There's a swell Western on, and the movie house is air-conditioned and cool—"

"Can't right now—I've got to mow this lawn," said Johnny.

"Oh, let it go. You can mow it later."

"You forget, Bobby. 'A Scout is Helpful.' Also 'A Scout is Obedient,' and—"

"I get it. I *did* forget. But I'll help you mow and then we can get through quicker. You know 'A Scout is Friendly.'"

"Swell. 'A Scout is Courteous,' so I agree. That is, in case you will take part of the money Dad is giving me for this," laughed Johnny.

"Sure, I'll be glad to because 'A Scout is Thrifty,'" quoted Bobby.

Between them they finished the lawn in half the time. Then Johnny said, "We will have to take a shower and get cleaned up."

"But that will take time," protested Bobby.

"'A Scout is Clean,'" reminded Johnny.

"And 'A Scout is Brave' and 'has courage to face danger in spite of fear, and—'"

"Cut it, and come on," said Johnny. The two boys took a shower and then, after Johnny obtained his mother's permission, they were off to the movie.

On the way Johnny said seriously, "You know, Bobby, we kidded a little, but the Scout Law is a great thing, isn't it?"

"It sure is. You can follow what it says in almost everything that comes up during the day and not go wrong. Yes, it is great!"

The Scout Law is one of the most important parts of the Scout Code. With the Scout Oath, the Scout Motto, and the Scout Slogan it includes the ideals of some of the most famous codes in the world's history—the Athenian Oath, the Mayflower Compact, the Declaration of Independence, and the code of the knights of the Middle Ages. It applies to nearly every happening in the Scout's daily life.

The Scout Oath and Law are part of the rules of the game of Scouting. The Scout Law consists of twelve points:

1. A SCOUT IS TRUSTWORTHY. A Scout's honor is to be trusted. If he were to violate his honor by telling a lie, or by cheating, or by not doing exactly a given task, when trusted on his honor, he may be directed to hand over his Scout Badge.

2. A SCOUT IS LOYAL. He is loyal to all to whom loyalty is due—his Scout leader, his home, and parents and country.

3. A SCOUT IS HELPFUL. He must be prepared at any time to save life, help injured persons, and share the home duties. He must do at least one Good Turn to somebody every day.

4. A SCOUT IS FRIENDLY. He is a friend to all and a brother to every other Scout.

5. A SCOUT IS COURTEOUS. He is polite to all, especially to women, children, old people, and the weak and helpless. He must not take pay for being helpful or courteous.

6. A SCOUT IS KIND. He is a friend to animals. He will not kill nor hurt any living creature needlessly, but will strive to save and protect all harmless life.

7. A SCOUT IS OBEDIENT. He obeys his parents, Scoutmaster, Patrol Leader, and all other duly constituted authorities.

8. A SCOUT IS CHEERFUL. He smiles whenever he can. His obedience to orders is prompt and cheery. He never shirks nor grumbles at hardships.

9. A SCOUT IS THRIFTY. He does not wantonly destroy property. He works faithfully, wastes nothing, and makes the best use of his opportunities. He saves his money so that he may pay his own way, be generous to those in need, and helpful to worthy causes. He may work for pay but must not receive tips for courtesies or Good Turns.

10. A SCOUT IS BRAVE. He has the courage to face danger in spite of fear and to stand up for the right against the coaxings of friends or the jeers or threats of enemies, and defeat does not down him.

11. A SCOUT IS CLEAN. He keeps clean in body and thought, stands for clean speech, clean sport, clean habits, and travels with a clean crowd.

12. A SCOUT IS REVERENT. He is reverent toward God. He is faithful in his religious duties, and respects the convictions of others in matters of custom and religion.

Two Scouts follow the Scout Law

When a Scout takes the Scout Oath, it is his promise to play the game according to the rules laid down in the Scout Law. It is a solemn promise that he makes. This is the Scout Oath or Promise:

"On my honor I will do my best:

"To do my duty to God and my country, and to obey the Scout Law;

"To help other people at all times;

"To keep myself physically strong, mentally awake, and morally straight."

See ATHENIAN OATH, CITIZENSHIP, SCOUT CODE, SCOUT MOTTO, SCOUT SLOGAN.

Scout Participation. Part of the Scout requirements for advancement in rank. It means that the Scout actually does his share in Patrol and Troop activities. Participation means that the Scout has been present at meetings and hikes, has faithfully performed the duties which were given him, and has tried to live up to what was expected of him by his Scoutmaster and Patrol Leader. It also means the way the Scout in his contacts with other people is courteous, helpful and friendly, respecting other people's property, and helping protect his country's natural resources. See ADVANCEMENT, SCOUT OATH AND LAW.

Scout Salute. The official salute of the Boy Scouts of America, used by uniformed Scouts in saluting the Flag of the United States and in approaching and leaving a Scout leader. The salute is given with the right hand, the three middle fingers straight, with the thumb covering the nail of the little finger. The hand in vertical position is brought smartly and smoothly to the head, palm sideways, until the fore-

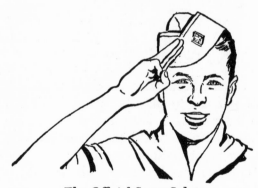

The Official Scout Salute

finger touches the hat, or head, above the right eye. It is then snapped down quickly and smoothly. See FLAG CODE, SCOUT SIGN.

Scout Sign. A sign given when the Scout repeats the Scout Oath and Law and also used by Scouts as a recognition signal. It is made by raising the right hand, palm

forward, upper forearm straight and out to the side. The three middle fingers are upward, and the thumb covers the nail of the little finger. See SCOUT OATH AND LAW, SCOUT SALUTE.

The Scout Sign is a recognition signal

Scout Slogan. "Do a Good Turn Daily." See GOOD TURN, SCOUT OATH AND LAW, SCOUT SPIRIT.

Scout Spirit. One of the requirements for advancement in Scouting. The Scout must satisfy his leaders that he does his best in everyday life to live up to the Scout Motto, the Scout Oath and Law, and the Scout Slogan. See SCOUT MOTTO, SCOUT OATH AND LAW, SCOUT SLOGAN.

Scribe. The keeper of the records or log of the Patrol or Troop. The best Scribes are those who can tell the history of the Unit in the most lively form on pages that look neat and orderly. Some Scribes illustrate their records with drawings of their own and with photographs. See LOG.

Sea Explorer. It was hot and dry. The Nebraska sun beat down on a parched, dusty, and shallow bowl. There was no water—neither stream nor lake—anywhere to be seen.

Off for a canoe trip at summer camp

At the edge of the dry bowl a group of Sea Explorers, dressed in their white uniforms, had unloaded two sailboats from a trailer. They were busy stepping the masts and rigging the sails. The mess detail already had a fire going and was cooking navy beans and brown bread.

"Looks like a fine day for sailing!" exclaimed one of the Sea Explorers.

"Yes, it's sure going to be great!" agreed another, gazing out over the arid scene.

Just then a member of the National Explorer Committee, who had been driving across the state, came up. He could hardly believe what he saw. He did not know whether to laugh or to shake his head in pity. He got out of his car.

"I want to compliment you fellows on your fine spirit," he said. "You are true Sea Explorers. How I wish you had some water!"

"Water, sir!" piped up a redheaded Ordinary Seaman. "Look back over those hills, sir. See those black clouds?"

"Yes," replied the committeeman. "But what of them?"

"Why, it's raining in the hills. The creeks are filling up. In an hour this bowl will be a two-mile lake. If we are lucky, it won't dry up for a couple of days."

Sure enough, the water soon began to tumble into the bowl. With a shout of joy the Sea Explorers launched their boats. There was fine sailing that day on the Nebraska prairie.

Not all Sea Explorers have to wait for such occasions. By way of contrast, many live near the ocean or on lakes and rivers and have fine sailing and boating whenever they want it.

Sea Exploring has attracted thousands of older Scouts and young men. Seamanship, sea lore, and Scouting ideals combine to make Sea Exploring popular on the coasts, waterways, and even the prairies.

First termed Sea Scouting, Sea Exploring began in 1912, two years after the Boy Scouts of America was incorporated. It was the first branch of the Explorer program and was open to all young men of fifteen and older. Now any young man may be a Sea Explorer at fourteen.

Four major activity fields are offered in Sea Exploring:

1. *Outdoor.* This includes cruises, wilderness expeditions, high adventures, and other activities requiring the skills of the seaman and outdoorsman.

2. *Social.* The lighter side of Sea Exploring with parties, "date" cruises, "stags," formal Bridges of Honor and Sea Explorer Balls, and such activities involving the courtesies and social skills of getting along well with others.

3. *Service.* This includes Emergency Service training, ways of helping other people, and projects serving the neighborhood and community, which require an understanding of participating citizenship.

4. *Vocational.* Exploration of occupations and hobbies leading to technical skills and lifelong occupations, through the Merit Badge Plan.

After the Sea Explorer's induction, a formal but brief ceremony, he is assigned to a Crew. A number of Crews make a Ship. The official dress uniform of the Sea Explorer may be either blue wool or white duck, whichever style has been adopted by the Ship. An embroidered strip, lettered "Sea Explorers, BSA," is worn over the right breast and a Sea Explorer emblem on the right sleeve.

Ranks in Sea Exploring are Apprentice, Ordinary, Able, and Quartermaster, the highest. The commissioned leaders in the Sea Explorer Ship are the Skipper or Ship Advisor, and one or more Mates or Assistant Ship Advisors. There are also three or more Ship Committeemen.

Sea Explorers thrill to the joy of boating and sailing

The Junior Leaders of a Ship are the Boatswain (Bo's'n) or Senior Crew Leader, the Boatswain's Mate or Deputy Senior Crew Leader, Crew Leaders, Assistant Crew Leaders, Yeomen, and Purser. See BOATSWAIN, BOY SCOUTS OF AMERICA, KNOTS, NAVIGATION, SEAMANSHIP, SEA PROMISE, SHIP (SEA EXPLORER), SHOOTING THE SUN, UNIFORMS.

Seamanship. Skill in navigation. It is the practical and noble art of rigging and working a ship and being able to navigate it. See NAVIGATION, SEA EXPLORER, SHIPS.

Sea Promise. A promise taken by the Sea Explorer. He pledges:

"As a Sea Explorer I promise to do my best—

"1. To guard against water accidents.

"2. To know the location and proper use of the life saving devices on every boat I board.

"3. To be prepared to render aid to those in need.

"4. To seek to preserve the Motto of the Sea, 'Women and Children First.'" See SEA EXPLORER.

Second Class Scout. The second rank in Boy Scouting. See BOY SCOUT.

Semaphore Signals. Signals made with two flags, one held in each hand. They may also be made with the arms. See SIGNALS.

Senior Crew Leader. The elected general chairman of an Explorer Unit. The Senior Crew Leader conducts all business meetings not in charge of someone else. He appoints committees, and all plans are cleared through him. He works closely with the Unit Advisor. See ADVISOR, EXPLORER.

Senior Patrol Leader. One of the most important positions of leadership in the Troop. The office is open to any First Class Scout (or Explorer equivalent) who has strong character, is proficient in Scouting, and has marked ability as a leader. He performs such Troop administrative and executive duties as are assigned to him by the Scoutmaster. See FIRST CLASS SCOUT, PATROL LEADER, TROOP LEADERS' COUNCIL.

Service to Others. See CITIZENSHIP, GOOD TURN.

Sextant. See SHOOTING THE SUN.

Shelters. Give the Scout his axe, knife, and poncho, and he will not find it hard to

The Adirondack shelter

provide himself with a comfortable shelter for the night when on the trail. Even without the poncho he can make his shelter from bark or other natural materials.

There are many kinds of shelters and they range from tents to emergency or wilderness shelters in caves or tunnels under fallen mountain boulders. Or a shelter may be a log cabin, or an Adirondack shelter.

The lean-to is one of the best forms of shelter for small parties of Scouts in the woods. The lean-to reached its highest state of devopment in the Adirondacks. There are a variety of ways of building the

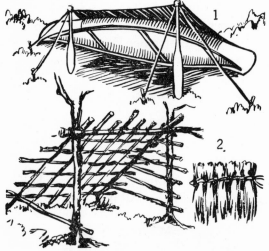

1. A canoe shelter   2. A thatch shelter

Adirondack shelter. Usually all the logs are notched together so that the walls are built entirely without nails, the front ends being firmly supported by short crosspieces. The roof beams are notched into the wall logs and support a roof which should be made of split shakes.

The projecting overhang front is an important feature, as this keeps the rain from driving in and helps the draft of the fire by carrying the smoke past the front of the lean-to instead of letting it eddy into the interior.

The log house is typical of the life of our pioneer ancestors, and the Scout learns how to build one.

The foundation is important. The Scout makes a foundation of stone, rising six inches or more above the ground, so that the bottom logs are kept dry. He first peels the logs. The logs of the lowest tier form the sills on which the floor is supported. The floor beams are held in place by

notches cut in the sills. The walls are then laid up, log upon log, each log being notched so as to fit closely on its neighbor.

When the log walls are up, roof beams and ridgepole are put in place in notches cut in the upper sides of the wall of logs. When a modern shingle or tarpaper roof is used, rafters are laid across the beams, and the roofing material fastened to the boards.

Shelters for the most part are coverings which can be carried easily by one person or can be constructed by him from Nature's supplies. The shelter for the backwoodsman was the lean-to; for the Indian on the march and the cowboy, the wickiup; and for the soldier the Army pup tent.

The Scout or Explorer constructs many types of overnight shelters from his shelter tarp. For this he uses 36-inch tarpaulin material. He uses three pieces, each 9 feet long, to make a square tarp. He employs four pieces, each 9 feet long, for a rectangular tarp. When the pieces are sewed together, he can make a variety of shelters.

With these handy pieces of tarpaulin or airplane cloth the Scout is assured of something that will keep out rain and cold and protect him from snakes and insects.

By folding his rectangular tarp he can make a *flattop tent*, using poles made from dead limbs or branches. He can also construct a *baker tent, half-pyramid tent, triangle tent, trail tent, or hammock tent,* the latter a real luxury in camp.

The square tarp is folded to form the *forester's tent,* which can be put up with a single pole; the *one-boy forester's tent,* which has two front-door flaps; or the *gypsy tent* or wigwam, which is made with poles bent over and lashed together and which looks like the top of a covered wagon.

The *canoe shelter* is a two-boy shelter arrangement made with the canoe and poncho. The canoe is kept in a slanting position by using the two paddles to act as braces, thus tilting the canoe to form a roof. The *poncho shelter* is a one-boy shelter. The poncho is laid over a ridgepole and staked down on each side. See CAMPING (ADVENTURE), HIKING TECHNIQUES, PONCHO, TENTS.

Shields (Indian). A project in Indian handicraft. Rawhide is stretched over a frame of thin, green branches, with arm

Scouts make and decorate Indian shields

straps in the back. Indian shields are colored and decorated with feathers and horsehair. Imitation shields, for ornamental purposes, are made from wallboard and decorated like regular shields. The rawhide used by Plains Indians in making their shields was from the buffalo and was heated over a fire to thicken it. See INDIAN HANDICRAFT.

Ships. Large seagoing vessels of any rig, but the name is more properly applied to those with three masts, having square sails on each mast. To be absolutely correct, a ship in the old days had to have a fidded topmast. However, sloops, barks, barken-

tines, and schooners were commonly termed ships, and today the term is also applied to vessels powered with engines. See SEA EXPLORER.

Ship (Sea Explorer). A chartered Unit of at least five Explorers, specializing in a seamanship program. A Ship is made up of a number of Crews. See SEA EXPLORER.

Shooting the Sun. Measuring the altitude of the sun or other heavenly body with a sextant. By computing this altitude with known Greenwich time and with certain facts found in the *Nautical Almanac,* the navigator is enabled to find his latitude and longitude, or position at sea. The sun is always shot at noon. Sea Explorers are schooled in this nautical science. See NAVIGATION, SEA EXPLORER.

Using the sextant to "shoot the sun"

Signals. Halfway up the mountain the members of the Silver Fox Patrol stopped for a brief rest. They had left their base camp in the valley two hours before and were going to camp on the mountaintop that night.

"I can hardly wait for supper," said one Scout.

"Yes, those pork chops are going to taste mighty good," said another.

Scouts use the Morse code in wigwagging

"Each of us get two, don't we?" a third Scout asked the Grubmaster, who was sitting apart, looking a little glum.

The Grubmaster did not answer. He looked away over the valley below. Then he turned toward the others and blurted out, "Fellows, you are going to hate me—I forgot those pork chops."

A chorus of howls went up.

"We'll have to go back and get them!" exclaimed one Scout.

"No, we won't," replied the Patrol Leader. "The Lone Wolf Patrol hasn't left camp yet. We will signal them to get the pork chops out of the cooler and bring them along."

So one of the Scouts tied his neckerchief to a stick, and another took off his mess-kit

lid and polished it with a cloth. The two went to a point of rock from which they could see the base camp. The Scout with the mess-kit lid caught the reflection of the sun with it and flashed the beam toward the camp. Soon there was an answering signal from below.

The Scout with the neckerchief on the stick spelled out the message in International Morse Code by wigwagging: "Forgot our pork chops. Look in cooler and bring them."

Finally came back the glad news that the pork chops were on the way.

Signals are signs agreed upon, or understood, and used to convey information, especially at a distance. They are fun, but they are more than that. Many times they save work, and they may save a life.

Signals are important in Scouting. Most of them are based on the International Morse Code, which is simply various arrangements of short and long intervals of sound, silence, light, or sight.

The Indians and early pioneers sent messages over long distances by means of signals which were previously agreed upon. The Scout uses many of these same signal methods but employs the International Morse Code with them.

By *heliographs* the Scout can send this code in flashes of sunlight. By *blinker* he can send it in flashes of artificial light. The same is true of *wigwagging*, in which the single flag is dipped to the sender's right to make a "short" or dot, and to the left to make a "long" or dash.

The International Morse Code can be sent, too, by a bugle, whistle, or dinner horn, as well as by many other means. There was a case in World War I when two American prisoners, tied up in a dark room and closely guarded, communicated their plan of escape to each other in long and short breaths.

Smoke signals are used by the Scout much as the Indians used them. Long and short puffs of smoke are sent up by means of a blanket raised and lowered over a smudge fire. See DISTRESS SIGNALS, FIELD SIGNALS, INTERNATIONAL MORSE CODE, PROCEDURE SIGNS, RADIO.

Silver Antelope. An annual award made by the National Council for noteworthy service to boyhood by a registered Scouter within one of the twelve Regions of the country. The symbol is a miniature Silver Antelope.

Silver Beaver. An annual award to Scouters made by the National Council for noteworthy service to boyhood by a registered Scouter within a Council. The symbol is a miniature Silver Beaver.

Silver Buffalo. An annual award made by the National Council for noteworthy service to boyhood of a national or international character, outside the regular line of duty, directly to or independent of the Boy Scouts of America. The symbol is a miniature Silver Buffalo.

Siple, Dr. Paul. The Scout who went with Admiral Byrd to the South Pole. Paul Siple became interested in science through his Merit Badge work as a Boy Scout, and later became an expert naturalist. He made two expeditions with Admiral Byrd to the Antarctic regions, and is now rated as one of the nation's leading scientific explorers. See BYRD.

Skiing. A winter sport popular with Scouts who live in regions where there is plenty of snow. Explorers sometimes use skis on winter expeditions. Skiing is a Merit Badge subject. See EXPLORER, MERIT BADGES.

Skish. A fisherman's game played with regular bait or fly-casting tackle. Ten targets, consisting of as many round rings or disks, not to exceed thirty inches in diameter, are placed at random in a pool of water and anchored at distances unknown to the caster. Two casts are allowed at each target. Scouts find this game a splendid means of improving casting technique, accuracy, and distance judging. See FISHING.

Smoke Signals. See SIGNALS.

Snake Bite. See FIRST AID.

Snakes. See REPTILES.

Snowhouse. The igloo of the Eskimo. This is a good dwelling in snow country and, if properly made, is warm and comfortable.

The snowhouse can be warm and comfortable

The snowhouse is constructed from packed or drifted snow. Snow is sufficiently packed when footprints are barely visible on it. The snow is then cut into blocks.

The first row of blocks is laid in a circle. These foundation blocks are then sliced off slantingly, so that when other blocks are laid on them they are built up in a spiral fashion. The snowhouse is dome-shaped, with an entrance which is tunneled beneath the wall.

Snowshoes. Supports for walking over snow, made of a frame with a network of

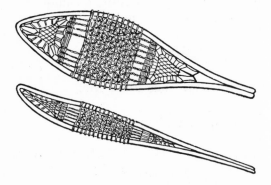

Snowshoes are used on soft snow

sinew, rawhide, or other material. Snowshoes can be used on light, fluffy snow which will not support skis.

There are many types of snowshoes, but the average model for a 150-pound person is about forty-two inches long and thirteen inches wide, with a pointed tail and slightly turned-up tip. Simple snowshoes can be made of barrel staves.

Soap Carving. An art project for Cub Scouts. Small figures are carved out of ordinary soap. See CUB SCOUTS.

Soil and Water Conservation. Without fertile soil, America would have no crops, no cattle, no food. The Scout conservationist knows methods of preventing soil erosion and making it fertile. He knows how to rotate crops. He shows others these methods in projects and in Merit Badge Shows, Troop Displays, and at school. He watches the water in nearby streams and reports any poor conditions to his State Conservation Commission. He, with his Troop, undertakes conservation projects which result in clean streams and finer fishing. He makes exhibits showing food chains for fish. He works with his State Conservation Service. See CONSERVATION PLEDGE, MERIT BADGES, SOIL CONSERVATION SERVICE.

Soil Conservation Service. A government department concerned chiefly with saving the soil. It directs erosion-control activities and practices. See CONSERVATION, SOIL AND WATER CONSERVATION.

Songs. Two miles more to go. These last miles were going to be tough. Doug's pack was becoming heavier and heavier. His feet were like lead. He wanted to sit down and rest and rest. . . .

Songs make the miles go faster

Then from up in front came the voice of the Cheermaster:

"Let's have a song, fellows."

"Yeah, the 'Good Old Open Trail'!" shouted one of the Patrols.

"How about 'There's a Long, Long Trail A-winding'?"

But one Scout already had started singing "Hi Ho for Scouting, Oh." The others caught up the tune, and soon they were all singing merrily and in rhythm to their steps.

Doug started to sing, too. He would never know how it happened, but those last two miles were the best part of the hike. He did not feel tired any longer. His pack was not heavy and he walked along as fresh and lively as at the start.

One song led to another. The Scouts came into camp singing their own Patrol Song, a tune which all the boys liked and with words about their own Patrol.

Nor were Doug and the others too tired that night around the campfire when someone suggested, "Let's have a song!"

The boys were off again.

Whether they are good singers or not, all boys like to sing. When they join their voices in singing with the Patrol or Troop, they feel closer together as friends and comrades. Singing is a great builder of morale, of unity, and of tradition, especially when boys have a song for their own Patrol and Troop.

It is said that the only "complete" Patrol or Troop is a singing Patrol or Troop. And each such Unit has a treasury of songs from which fun, laughter, good fellowship, and fond memories can be drawn at the proper time. See CHANTEYS.

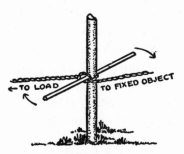

A Spanish windlass is a useful emergency tool

Spanish Windlass. A rough-and-ready method of using a rope and poles to shift a load or haul a car out of soggy ground. The Scout fastens one end of a rope to the load and the other to a tree or similar fixed object. One Scout then holds a short, strong stick vertically against the center of the rope, while other Scouts insert a smaller stick into the bight of the rope, and use it to revolve the upright stick and thus to pull up the load.

Special Events. Activities of the District or Local Council, usually involving all the Troops or other Units in the area. These activities may include Camporees, state and county fairs and expositions, pilgrimages to historic shrines, winter carnivals, Council campfires, community service, and community programs. See CAMPOREE, LOCAL COUNCIL.

Splices. Types of ropework in which two ropes or two parts of the same rope are joined together by interweaving the strands. Splicing is important in Scouting for lengthening ropes, repairing injured ropes, forming eyes in the ends of ropes, and finishing off the ends of ropes.

The simplest form of splicing is the *short splice*. This is commonly used when a rope is injured or broken and is to be joined back together, or where two ropes of the same size are to be joined. The strands of each end are unlaid and "married," and then the strands of each rope are tucked under and over those of the other rope.

The *long splice* is a more artistic splice in which long strands from each of the ropes are laid back into the ropes themselves. When a strand is laid back, it takes the place of a strand in the opposite rope. The strands are finally tucked, these tucks being scattered or staggered.

The *back splice* is used in finishing off the ends of ropes so that they will not fray.

137

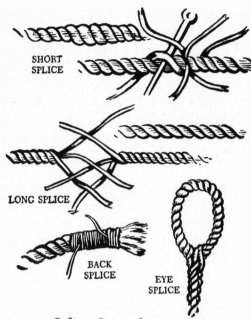

SHORT SPLICE

LONG SPLICE

BACK SPLICE

EYE SPLICE

Splices Scouts learn to use

The strands are first unlaid for a short distance and then formed into a crown knot. Then the ends of the strands are spliced back along the rope as in the short splice.

The *eye splice,* as usually made by the Scout, is called the *side splice* when used to splice one rope into another. It is used in forming a permanent loop or eye. In such a case the rope is bent back onto itself in a bight, and the loosened strands on the end are spliced into the body of the rope as in the short splice. See KNOTS, ROPEWORK.

Squadron. A chartered Air Explorer Unit of five or more Explorers specializing in aviation activities. It is composed of Crews. See AIR EXPLORER.

Stag Party. A party given by Explorers in honor of their employers, teachers, ministers, fathers, or favorite merchants. It is sometimes called "Bosses' Night."

Stalking. Scouts enjoy trailing wild life. With the Scout uniform for protective cov-

ering, and the ability to "freeze" (stay motionless), the ability to observe carefully, to go out and discover nature, they make expert stalkers. Stalking opens up new adventure in the outdoors and is a fascinating hobby. See TRACKING AND TRAILING, WHIFFLEPOOF.

Stamp Collections. See COLLECTIONS.

Star Charts. Maps of the sky showing the positions of the stars at various times of the year. See STARS.

Stars. Every star is a sun, most of them bigger than our own and so far away that their distance is measured in "light years." Light travels 186,000 miles per second, and that multiplied by the number of seconds in a year gives the number of miles in a "light year." The sun is only 93,000,000 miles from the Earth, but the nearest fixed star is over 200,000 times that distance.

Besides the stars, Scouts know the planets, of which the earth is one, which revolve around the sun. Other stars also have a system of planets.

The Scout learns the names of the planets and to find his way at night by the stars. The most valuable star for direction-finding is Polaris, the pole star, or, as it is usually called, the North Star. The Scout can locate this star by any one of four methods. One way is by the pointer stars of the big dipper (Ursa Major), which are in direct line with the North Star. The North Star can be lined up, too, with the two stars which are farthest apart in the head of the Dragon Star (Draco). A third method is to follow from the double star in the middle of the Big Dipper to the center of Cassiopeia. A fourth way is to locate it through the pointer stars in the Northern Cross (part of Cygnus).

However, the Scout can use any star to

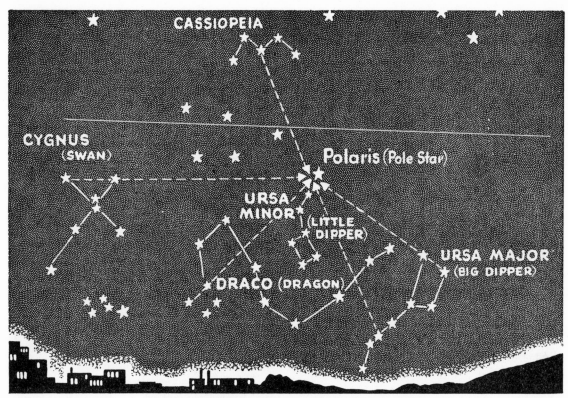

Scouts know how to use the stars to find directions

tell direction. He sights a particular star across the tops of two sticks, one long and one short, which are stuck in the ground. He watches the star for a few minutes. It appears to move.

If the star moves upward, the Scout knows he is facing a general easterly direction. If it moves downward, he is looking toward a westerly direction. If the star moves in an arc from right to left, he is facing in a general northerly direction. If it moves in a flat arc from left to right, the direction is southerly.

It is interesting to note that, except for the northerly direction, these same rules apply to the sun. If moving up, it is in the east; if in an arc from left to right, it is southerly; and if dropping down, it is in the western part of the heavens.

Star charts, which show a layout of the stars at different times of the year, are as important in many instances as are maps of the land. Sailors have long used stars to find their way across oceans, and air pilots use them today in navigating their aircraft.

Star Scout. The fourth rank in Scouting. To earn this rank the First Class Scout serves at least three months and meets requirements in Scout Spirit, Scout Participation, and Scoutcraft and Life Interests, including certain Merit Badges. See BOY SCOUT, FIRST CLASS SCOUT, MERIT BADGES.

Step Measuring. See JUDGING.

String Burning. A Scoutcraft project in which several teams participate. Two strings are stretched tightly between two vertical sticks by each team, with one string eighteen inches above the ground and the other twenty-four inches. Two

Scouts form a team. The team gathers wood, lays a fire beneath the strings, and

A contest of Scoutcraft skill

at a signal lights the fire. Only two matches are given each team. The team whose fire first burns through both strings has the highest score. See SCOUTCRAFT.

Sundial. A Scout can make a sundial out of two can tops this way: He takes the top of a can of beans, taps it till it is flat, and pastes a sundial clock on top. He cuts the shadow fin from another top, and folds it and inserts it in position.

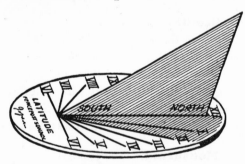

A home-made sundial

Survival Techniques. Basic training in skills that enable a person to live in the wilderness in emergency. Some plants provide food; others, good wood for fires. The Scout learns to make fishlines from bark and hooks from thorns. He can make rope from fiber and construct a snare to catch food. The Scout knows how to construct an emergency shelter and a ground bed, and to make fire by friction. He practices these skills in camp and on hikes.

He builds a nature trail and a demonstration area for practice. He trains himself physically to be strong, and mentally to be alert. He is prepared.

Survival techniques teach how to live in the wilderness. See FIRE BY FRICTION, GROUND BEDS, LOST!, NATURE CRAFTS, NATURE TRAIL, SHELTERS, WILD FOODS.

Swappin'. A Scout term for trading, especially at Jamborees. Scouts equipped with "swappin' bags" hung from their belts bargain with one another for various items such as neckerchief slides, whetstones, knives, noggins, and many other things.

The Scout is mainly interested in swappin' for articles which are from other countries or other localities. The only conditions in swappin' are that gadgets should be in keeping with the policies and best interests of Scouting and that no swappin' is done with the idea of making money. See JAMBOREE (WORLD).

Swimming. "Every Scout a Swimmer" is a Scout slogan. Thousands of boys are taught to swim in camp each summer. Swimming is a requirement for First Class rank. Safety measures are stressed in swimming, and in camps the "buddy plan" is used, by which Scouts swim in pairs and watch out for each other.

Swimming is a Merit Badge subject, and to earn his badge the Scout must be able to swim 150 yards in good form, using the side stroke, elementary back stroke, and breast stroke. He must also demonstrate a rescue in water. See BUDDY PLAN, LIFE SAVING, MERIT BADGES.

Tenderfoot Scout. The first rank in Scouting. To become a Tenderfoot Scout a boy must be at least eleven years old and must meet certain requirements in Scout Spirit, Scout Participation, and Scoutcraft, including knowing the Scout Oath and Law.

When he has completed the requirements, he is formally received into the Troop at a special Investiture ceremony and the Scoutmaster gives him his Tenderfoot Badge. See ADVANCEMENT, BOY SCOUT, CANDIDATE SCOUT, INVESTITURE CEREMONIES, SCOUTCRAFT, SCOUT PARTICIPATION, SCOUT SPIRIT.

Tents. Outdoor shelters usually made of canvas, supported by poles, and fastened by cords tied to pegs driven into the ground.

There the three types of tents. One is the *wedge* or *A tent*, which includes wall and pup tents. The second type is the *pyramid tent*, which includes the Indian tepee. The third type is the *open-front tent*, such as the forester, baker, and trail tents.

Scouts take pride in making their own tents, and the tents of one Patrol or Troop may be of different colors or decoration, or they may be all alike.

For instance, in a recent National Jamboree, Scouts began working months ahead

The forester tent is comfortable to live in

to construct their own particular type of tent, the *Jambo* or *Jamboree tent*. This tent was designed along the lines of Scout standards which had been followed for years.

The Jambo tent provided about thirty

141

square feet per camper, with room enough for the Scout to move about, stretch himself, and stand up. It was made of 20¼ yards of lightweight balloon cloth or top-grade unbleached muslin. Full instructions were given in ample time in *Boys' Life,* the Scout magazine, so that Scouts could complete such a tent for the Jamboree.

In camp a Scout spends more time in his tent than in any other one place. Out of twenty-four hours he sleeps in it from eight to nine hours, may take a rest in it after his lunch, and sometimes sits on the end of his bunk while he cooks his meals on the warming fire just outside the tent. He wants his tent as comfortable as he can make it.

The Scout pitches his tent on a slope so that the rainwater will run off, he shelters it from prevailing winds, and he is sure that enough water and wood are close at hand. He also watches out that the tent is not too near trees with dead branches which might break off and wreck it, or too near trees which might blow over in a storm. See CAMPING (LONG-TERM), SHELTERS.

Scouts use the Indian tepee

Tepee. The cone-shaped dwelling of the Plains Indians. Twelve or more long poles are arranged upright around a circle on the ground. Three are lashed together to form a pyramid and the others are leaned against these. Scouts use canvas as a covering and decorate their tepees in Indian style. See SHELTERS, TENTS.

Thrifty, A Scout Is. The ninth point of the Scout Law. "A SCOUT IS THRIFTY. He does not wantonly destroy property. He works faithfully, wastes nothing, and makes the best of his opportunities. He saves his money so he may pay his own way, be generous to those in need, and helpful to worthy objects. He may work for pay, but must not receive tips for courtesies or Good Turns." See GOOD TURN, SCOUT OATH AND LAW.

Thunderbird. See FIRE BY FRICTION.

Tin-Can and Wire Crafts. There was a knock at the back door. The housewife hastily wiped her hands and went to see who was there.

"Excuse me, ma'am," said a nice-looking youngster who was standing on the porch, hat in hand. "I wanted to ask you if I could have those two large tin cans and those coat hangers beside the garbage pail."

"Why, of course," responded the housewife. She started to close the door, but hestitated. Then she asked, "But what in the world do you want them for?"

"Well, you see, I am a Boy Scout—"

"You don't mean there is another scrap-metal campaign on?"

"Oh, no—nothing like that. I can use these things to make camping equipment."

"Well, you may certainly have them. But might I ask what you can possibly make out of tin cans and coat hangers?"

"Sure. My Patrol is going on a hike. We want to make a tin-can cooker, and these cans are just about the right size for it. And with the coat hangers we will make a grill, some fire tongs, a fork for roasting hot dogs, and—"

"Now just imagine! You can make all those things out of these cans and coat hangers? If you will wait a minute, I'll see if I can find you some more."

"No, thanks, these are enough."

Examples of Scout-made tin and wire work

The housewife was becoming more and more interested.

"And you use these things we throw out! Well, I must say that is being thrifty. But, now that I think of it, when my husband and I were in New Mexico a few years ago, I remember how the Indians out there made lamps, mirror frames, candlesticks and even roofs for their houses out of old tin cans. Do the Scouts teach you to make a lot of things?"

"Yes, they do. We can make candleholders, too, and soap dishes, lanterns, paper holders—oh, a lot of things from old tin cans and bailing wire and coat hangers."

Yes, and with tin cans the Scout can make a stewpot, frying pan, double boiler, and, as the boy said, a "lot of things." He must find the right-size cans for his various projects. They are first sterilized in boiling

water for fifteen minutes and then worked into shape with tin snips, pliers, and a file. The coat hangers are worked after the paint has been scraped or burned off, and can be twisted into many useful shapes. See HANDICRAFTS; THRIFTY, A SCOUT IS.

Tom-Toms. See INDIAN HANDICRAFT.

Topographical Map. See MAPS, U.S. GEOLOGICAL SURVEY MAPS.

Totem. The early American Indians had totems. The Indian totem usually was an animal thought of as an emblem of a person or clan. Scouts have totems, too. No Scout Patrol is without one of these emblems, and it is used on the Patrol flag, the Patrol medallions the boys wear on their Scout shirts, in decorating the den, and to mark all Patrol equipment. Patrol totems are usually animals, too—but not always. Scouts carve totem poles giving the history of their Patrol or Troop. Sometimes they have a totem pole contest. See FLAGS, PATROL.

Scout totems follow Indian designs

Tracking and Trailing. In the middle of the night there came a weird scream. Then the sound of scuffling and a low moan. Finally there was a noise of something crashing through the brush.

143

Half the Scouts in the camp bolted upright in their beds. They imagined all sorts of things. Some were frightened and crawled back under covers, pulling them over their heads. Hardly anyone slept the rest of the night.

The next morning several Scouts were trying to solve the mystery. They found some broken bushes and some animal tracks.

But one Scout, who had real skill and a knowledge of woodlore, was going about the investigation in a careful way. He scraped some hairs from a rock. He looked at the tracks in the soft earth. Then he walked off into the brush. After a time he returned. He was smiling. "Nothing to worry about, fellows," he said. "A raccoon was on his way to the little spring there to get a drink. I found his tracks leading that way. But a bear caught up with him. The raccoon screamed. The bear knocked him over with one swipe of his big paw. That's when we heard the low moan. Then the bear made off with the raccoon through the brush."

This is a true story and it is recounted in the *Handbook for Boys*. It illustrates how a wise Scout solved a mystery by careful observation, knowledge of woodlore, and a little detective work.

For trailing and tracking are woodland "detecting." No Sherlock Holmes examines a cigar ash more carefully to determine the brand than the expert tracker examines the trail signs and marks in identifying and following his quarry.

In the old days both white and Indian scouts could "read sign" that meant nothing to those who had no experience. They called this "trailing or following sign." "Sign" was the evidence left behind by man or beast. Cowboys called it "riding sign," and they could trail horses, cattle, or badmen by following their "sign."

It is an exciting game. In tracking animals, for instance, the Scout must know four things. He must know all about the animals themselves. He must know how to find their tracks and other sign which they leave behind them. He must know how to follow these tracks and sign and not be misled. Then he must know how to stalk the animals so that he can get close to them to take a picture or study them.

The good tracker must learn to observe. He must be on the alert always for natural signs. A pebble turned over or a blade of grass bent down the wrong way means something to him.

It is important to know how to look. The expert, in walking along, sweeps his eyes in a semicircle ahead of him. This semicircle is not large, say about ten feet. He divides the semicircle into distances ahead of him.

The first sweep of his eyes, say from left to right, covers an area of six to eight feet ahead of him. Then he turns his eyes from the right to the left to take in an area of about thirty feet. In another sweep of his eyes he sees everything up to fifty feet. He always wants to know what is going on at least that distance ahead of him.

If the Scout is looking for animal tracks, he tries to walk against the sun. Then the shadows are longer and the tracks look deeper.

Trail signs or trail markers offer good practice in observation. These are signs made by another Scout who has gone ahead. Such signs are made with sticks laid in a certain way, or grass tied in knots and bent over, or they may be made with the whifflepoof, which is a track-making device.

In trailing or stalking, the Scout moves along silently and slowly. He learns how to walk on any type of ground without mak-

Keen-eyed Scouts follow a trail through the wilderness

ing a noise. In grass or leaves he steps with the heel down first and then the toe, slowly and easily. On hard ground the toe comes down first and then the heel. The balance is always kept on the back foot.

In stalking, the Scout uses tracking skills

The Scout must always keep cover and try not to be seen. In low shrubbery he crouches and in the grass he crawls or creeps along. He moves from bush to bush and from tree to tree. If a wind is blowing and the grass is moving, he can safely move the grass himself. But if there is no wind, he must be careful not to move the grass, as this will give away his position at once.

In taking cover he observes his background. He must be careful not to form a silhouette of any part of his body. He must blend into his background.

Wind is important. In approaching animals the Scout should go upwind, with the wind blowing from the animal toward him. Then the animal cannot smell him.

"Freezing" is important and an art. No matter what his position, the Scout must learn to freeze instantly into it, not moving a muscle and scarcely breathing. He must remain in this position until it is safe to move again. Freezing may save his life.

Many old-timers, in recounting "b'ar stories," have told how when a bear came upon them they remained rigid, never moving, even if the bear walked over them.

In following human tracks a Scout knows that, if another Scout is running, only the ball of his foot touches the ground. If the quarry is trying to throw off his trailer and is walking backward, his steps will be shorter. If he is carrying anything heavy, his heel marks are deeper. If he tries to fool his trailer by walking a short distance in a stream, he usually will come out on the same side of the stream that he went in.

In trailing and tracking, then, the Scout learns to use his eyes, his ears, his nose, and even his fingers. See STALKING, TRACKS (ANIMAL), TRAIL SIGNS, WHIFFLEPOOF, WOODLORE.

Tracks (Animal). The animal leaves his trade-mark or seal on the earth when he walks. Some animals are of the flatfoot variety, like the beaver, porcupine, bear, and man. Cats, dogs, and wolves are known as "toe walkers," for they walk on their toes. Hoofed animals, such as deer, are "toenail walkers."

In the forest and wilderness it is important to be able to recognize the tracks of various animals, including those of birds as well as of mammals. Scouts, in nature crafts, make casts directly from the tracks so that they can have records of them. See NATURE CRAFTS, TRACKING AND TRAILING.

Trail Breads. See BISCUITS, BREAD ON A STICK.

Trail Signs. Markers set up along a trail to show someone else the way, or leave a message. These signs may be scratch marks in the dirt, sticks set in a certain way, grasses knotted and bent, or rocks piled in a certain order. See TRACKING AND TRAILING, WHIFFLEPOOF.

Transporting Injured Persons. See CARRIES.

Trees. Woody plants with a single trunk, which reach ten feet or more in height. There are many kinds of trees, ranging from the softwood to the hardwood varieties. Willow and cottonwood trees grow near water, while pines and cedars grow on higher ground.

Trees are the homes of many animals—birds, mammals, and insects. They provide man with building materials in the form of logs and lumber. Their bark is used for many purposes. Some trees bear nuts, berries, or beans which are good eating. See CONSERVATION, FORESTS, NATURE TRAIL, TREES, CARE OF.

Trees, Care of. Millions of trees are set out yearly by Scouts. Many Troop camps and Council camps have taken advantage of the low cost at which young trees may be obtained from the state conservation departments to plant trees at their camps.

Scouts aid in fighting forest fires

Scouts help preserve forests and protect trees in many ways. They are careful to prevent forest fires by keeping their campfires always under control, and by putting them out carefully when they leave a campsite. Those who live in forest areas are always ready to aid local wardens or conservation agencies in fighting forest fires. Scouts, too, are careful not to chop down living trees except in emergencies. See CONSERVATION, FORESTS, TREES.

Trek Cart. A cart with four wheels, usually made by the Scouts themselves, in which they carry Patrol camping gear and equipment for a camping trip. Two Scouts pull the cart. When the Patrol reaches the campsite, camp is set up for the night, next day the trek cart is again loaded, and off the Patrol goes on further adventure.

Tribe. A group of Lone Scouts. See LONE SCOUT.

Troop. A chartered Unit of five or more Boy Scouts, made up of two or more Patrols. The leader is a man citizen, whose title is Scoutmaster. He has one or more Assistant Scoutmasters to help him. A Troop is operated by a sponsoring organization, such as a church or school or group of citizens. See CHARTER, PATROL, SCOUTMASTER.

Troop Camping. Camp—there's a thrill for every real boy! It gives freedom, fun, and adventure.

Troop Camping is the Scout way of camping. When the whole Troop goes camping together, with the Scoutmaster and other Troop leaders, the Scouts have the time of their lives. Each Scout has a job to do, and all work and learn and have fun together.

First the Troop decides upon a campsite, maybe at the Council camp, maybe on its

The swim at camp is a high spot of the day

own campsite. The campsite has three features of top importance—shelter, wood, water.

Shelter—protected from winds but fairly open; not too many trees, for they prevent the tents from drying out.

Water—a pure supply for drinking and swimming near the site.

Wood—enough for fuel and camp improvements.

The Troop camp is set up by Patrols, and usually each Patrol brings its own tents and camping equipment. The Scouts cook and eat by Patrols, and enjoy most of the program and camp activities by Patrols. Each Scout has his own personal equipment, too, and his own pack. The Scout travels light, takes a minimum of gear, but knows how to make himself comfortable.

The bugle wakes the camp. First comes breakfast, then clean-up. Then activities— nature study, hiking, signaling, orienteering—whatever the Scouts need to practice. Next, swimming—each Scout with his buddy, according to Scout safety practice. What an appetite the Scouts have when the cooks set out the lunch!

After clean-up and a rest period, there are hikes, exploration, archery, rope spinning, ball games, fishing, games, and other interesting things to do. Then perhaps another swim. By this time the Scouts are hungry again. How good dinner tastes out in the open!

The campfire session comes later, the flames leaping up, with songs, stunts, skits, laughter, and good fellowship.

Taps sound too soon. The fire is put out. Scouts go to bed. Lights out. Silence in the camp. The next morning—another glorious day of adventure and excitement.

Scouts have rigid standards of camping, and every Troop camp is expected to be up to standard, to give Scouts a safe, healthful, and happy experience in the open. See CAMPING (LONG TERM).

Troop Leaders' Council. The Patrol Leaders, the Senior Patrol Leader, Junior Assistant Scoutmasters, the Scoutmaster, and Assistant Scoutmasters make up the Troop Leaders' Council.

The Scoutmaster does not run the Troop by himself. He depends on the help of the Patrol Leaders and others in the Troop Leaders' Council.

The Troop Leaders' Council meets regularly to plan the Troop program, activities, camping, and the Good Turns of the Troop. Before attending such a meeting the Patrol Leader talks over matters with the members of his Patrol, and in this manner every boy has something to say about what the Troop shall do. See ASSISTANT SCOUTMASTER, JUNIOR ASSISTANT SCOUTMASTER, PATROL, PATROL LEADER, SCOUTMASTER, SENIOR PATROL LEADER, TROOP.

Troop Stunts. Stunts by Patrols or by individuals often form a part of the campfire period. These stunts may be short skits, improvised dramatics, Scoutcraft demonstrations, Indian ceremonies, or campfire challenge games. They are usually short, wholesome, and lively. See CAMPFIRE CEREMONIES, COUNCIL FIRE, SCOUTCRAFT.

Trustworthy, A Scout Is. The first point of the Scout Law, which reads: "A SCOUT IS TRUSTWORTHY. A Scout's honor is to be trusted. If he were to violate his honor by telling a lie, or by cheating, or by not doing exactly a given task, when trusted on his honor, he may be directed to hand over his Scout Badge." See SCOUT OATH AND LAW.

A tumpline helps support a back pack

Tumpline. A soft piece of leather worn across the forehead with two thongs for attaching the load or pack, to be carried on the back. The American Indians, who originated the device, called it a pack or portage strap. See PACKS (FOR CARRYING).

Uniforms. Scout uniforms are authorized by the Congress of the United States and are protected from unlawful use by an Act of Congress. The uniform has been designed with great care and is a constant reminder of the important things in Scouting—character, service, democracy, friendship, adventure, and citizenship.

Millions of boys and young men throughout the world wear the Scout uniform. While many speak different languages and have different customs, they are bound together by their uniform into a world brotherhood.

Boys and leaders of each branch of Scouting have a distinct uniform. The colors of the uniforms are as follows: Cub Scouts, blue and gold; Boy Scouts, khaki with red piping; Explorers, forest green with brown; Sea Explorers, navy blue or white; Air Explorers, sky blue with royal blue piping. On the uniform the Scout wears his badges of membership, office, rank, and award in the proper positions. The uniform bears the Official Seal of the Boy Scouts of America. See BADGES AND INSIGNIA, BOY SCOUT, EXPLORER, WORLD BROTHERHOOD OF SCOUTING.

Unknown Scout. The unidentified Scout of England who performed the Good Turn which brought Scouting to America. In Gilwell Park, England, international training center, stands a bronze buffalo, gift of the Boy Scouts of America, commemorating the event. See BOYCE.

U.S. Geological Survey Maps. Official maps issued by the U.S. Geological Survey, Department of the Interior, Washington, D.C. These maps are known as topographical maps, and they give detailed descriptions of particular places, or show the physical features of these places. The maps are made to different scales. Some are to a scale of 1:62,500, which means that one inch on the map equals 62,500 inches on level ground, or about one inch to the mile. The Scout learns how to use these maps to find his way. See MAPS.

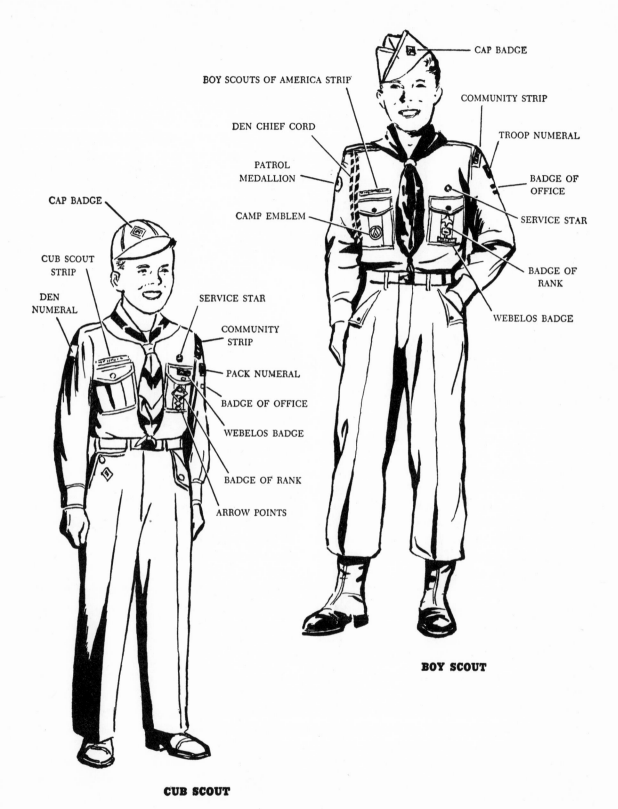

CAP BADGE

BOY SCOUTS OF AMERICA STRIP

DEN CHIEF CORD

PATROL MEDALLION

CAMP EMBLEM

CAP BADGE

COMMUNITY STRIP

TROOP NUMERAL

BADGE OF OFFICE

SERVICE STAR

BADGE OF RANK

WEBELOS BADGE

CAP BADGE

CUB SCOUT STRIP

DEN NUMERAL

SERVICE STAR

COMMUNITY STRIP

PACK NUMERAL

BADGE OF OFFICE

WEBELOS BADGE

BADGE OF RANK

ARROW POINTS

BOY SCOUT

CUB SCOUT

Each branch of Scouting has its special uniform (SEE ALSO NEXT PAGE)

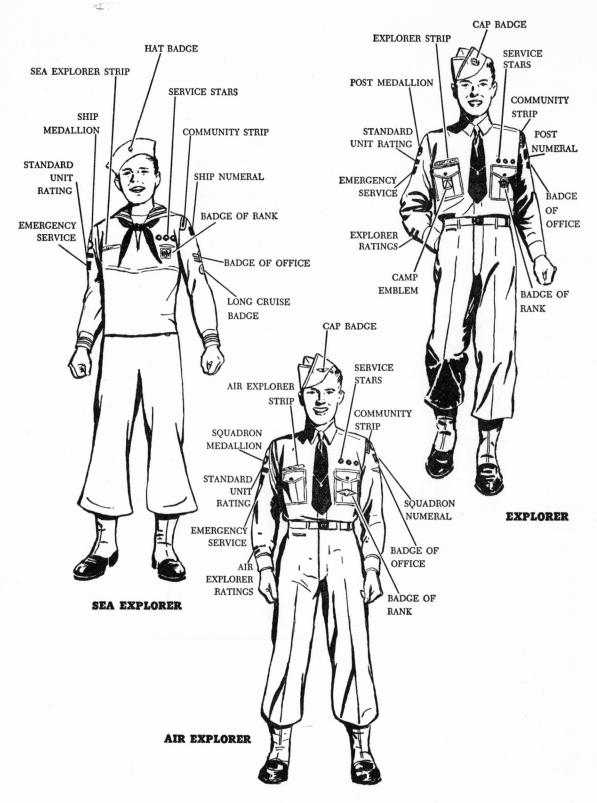

SEA EXPLORER STRIP
SHIP MEDALLION
HAT BADGE
STANDARD UNIT RATING
SERVICE STARS
COMMUNITY STRIP
EMERGENCY SERVICE
SHIP NUMERAL
BADGE OF RANK
BADGE OF OFFICE
LONG CRUISE BADGE

SEA EXPLORER

AIR EXPLORER STRIP
CAP BADGE
SERVICE STARS
COMMUNITY STRIP
SQUADRON MEDALLION
STANDARD UNIT RATING
EMERGENCY SERVICE
SQUADRON NUMERAL
AIR EXPLORER RATINGS
BADGE OF OFFICE
BADGE OF RANK

AIR EXPLORER

EXPLORER STRIP
CAP BADGE
SERVICE STARS
POST MEDALLION
COMMUNITY STRIP
STANDARD UNIT RATING
POST NUMERAL
EMERGENCY SERVICE
BADGE OF OFFICE
EXPLORER RATINGS
CAMP EMBLEM
BADGE OF RANK

EXPLORER

All badges and insignia have a special position on the uniform

V=W

Veteran Scout. A registered Explorer or Scouter who has been active in Scouting for at least ten years. There are special Veteran Badges for every five years of registered active service after ten. A Scout or Scouter who has five years of registered service as a Cub Scout, Boy Scout, Explorer, or Leader, or a combination of these, is eligible to receive a special certificate.

Veterans of Foreign Wars Scholarship. A $500 scholarship awarded annually by the Veterans of Foreign Wars to an Explorer for college study. The Explorer must have received an award for saving life from the National Court of Honor. The scholarship award is based on service to the community, to Scouting, and on scholarship and fine character. It is one of the most coveted honors in Scouting. See JAMES E. WEST CONSERVATION SCHOLARSHIP.

Wannigan. Scout lingo for food box.

Water Boiling. A Scoutcraft competition in which teams of four Scouts compete to make a pot of water boil. Each team must build a fire from wood the Scouts have chopped themselves. The water is usually in a two-quart pail, doused with one level tablespoon of soap powder. The team bringing the water to boil over the edge of the pot first, wins. All teams score according to achievements. This may be a one- or two-Scout contest also. See CAMPOREE, GAMES.

Water Carnival. A popular sport at Scout summer camps. The water carnival, or water meet, is usually held in the afternoon, with one or more entries from each Patrol. The program usually consists of a twenty-five-yard swim, fifty-yard swim, boat rescue, two-boy boat race, and four-boy canoe race, as well as other events. Water tilting, log rolling, sailboat racing, pageants, water polo, and many other exciting events may be added to make the carnival a gala occasion.

One popular event is the "Shirt Rescue." In this one boy swims out thirty feet and remains at this place in the water until rescued. The rescuer jumps into the water, carrying his shirt in his mouth, swims out, throws the end of his shirt to the "victim," and then tows him ashore.

In the Swim-Paddle-Run event the entrants swim fifty yards to a canoe, crawl in, paddle to shore, and then run to a marker fifty yards back on shore. See BOATS, CANOEING, SWIMMING.

Water (Drinking). The Scout makes sure that his drinking water is pure. When on hikes or in camp he purifies water from brooks, springs, rivers, and wells. He either boils his water for ten minutes and then pours it back and forth from one vessel to another to restore the air in it, or he uses water-purification tablets. See CAMPING (LONG-TERM), HIKING TECHNIQUES.

Waterproofing Tents. In making their own tents, Scouts waterproof the material. The material is first shrunk by being soaked an hour in hot, soapy water. After it is dry,

it is soaked again for four hours in a solution of one-half pound of alum dissolved in two quarts of hot water. Scouts sometimes use a commercial waterproofing mixture, being sure to follow directions carefully. See SHELTERS, TENTS.

Water Skiing. An exciting water sport in which one person on water skis is towed by a fast motorboat. This is a sport which requires considerable skill on the part of the skier. Water skiing is sometimes an event at Scout water carnivals. See WATER CARNIVAL.

Weather Predicting. If the Scout is going on a hike or a camping trip, he wants to know what the weather is going to be like. He learns to use barometers and other scientific instruments and to read the gov-

Patrols compete to show their skills at a water carnival

ernment meteorological, or weather, maps. Such maps are published by the U.S. Weather Bureau and are usually printed in the daily newspapers.

Scouts learn to know weather signs

Old-time weather lore is interesting but not always accurate. There is the story of the man who had employed a Canadian Indian guide while on a hunting trip. One day the guide advised against leaving camp, saying it was going to rain. Knowing the reputation of Indians for predicting weather, the man asked the guide how he knew it was going to rain. He expected to gain some wisdom in weather lore. "Radio Winnipeg!" promptly responded the guide.

However, there are plenty of natural signs by which weather can be predicted. Most woodsmen rely on clouds. Then, too, the woodsman depends upon his sense of hearing and his sight to foretell the weather. When distant objects "stand above the horizon" and are clear, rain can be expected. An unusual brightness and twinkling of the stars may mean wind. A "good hearing day," especially good hearing from the west quarter, means that rain will follow. A "poor hearing day" means a low humidity or moisture content of the air, and so fair weather may be expected. See CLOUDS.

Webelos. The Cub Scout "Indian Tribe," which receives its name from the words Wolf, Bear, Lion, and Scout. Akela is Chief of the Webelos.

The Cub Scout strives to earn his Webelos Badge—the highest rank in Cub Scouting—as this prepares him to enter a Scout Troop. He must be at least ten and one-half years of age and a Lion Scout, and show that he is prepared in the Tenderfoot Scout requirements. See AKELA, CUB SCOUT, HANDBOOK FOR BOYS, LION, TENDERFOOT SCOUT.

West, James E. (1878–1948). The first Chief Scout Executive, later Chief Scout. He was an outstanding youth leader recognized throughout the world for his vision and ability. He developed the Twelfth Scout Law and the first *Handbook for Boys*. See JAMES E. WEST CONSERVATION SCHOLARSHIP.

Whifflepoof. A piece of wood covered with nails driven into it about halfway. A Scout drags this device over the ground to

The whifflepoof is used to lay a trail

leave a trail which another Scout may follow in the practice of tracking and trailing. See STALKING, TRACKING AND TRAILING.

Whippings (Rope). Finishings for the ends of ropes to keep them from fraying. Stout twine or small line is wound around the end of the rope, and the ends of the

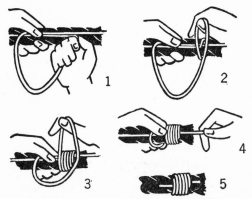

Five steps in whipping rope ends

twine or line tucked in. Sometimes the whipping is put on with a sailor's palm and needle. The palm is a leather protection for the hand. See KNOTS, ROPEWORK.

Whittling. Carving, shaping, or otherwise cutting by hand with a knife. Whittling is an art, and with his knife the Scout can make many things from wood, such as whistles, totem poles, and camp gadgets. See KNIFE.

Wigwagging. See INTERNATIONAL MORSE CODE, SIGNALS.

Wilderness Camping. See CAMPING (ADVENTURE).

Wild Foods. Two Scouts were sitting on the grass beneath a shade tree. They had been talking of many things and now they were silent, daydreaming of a happy life on a desert island or in the wilderness.

"But I guess I would miss Mother's apple pies," finally remarked Doug, the older Scout, looking toward the kitchen from which came the smell of a fresh-baked pie.

"Oh, I don't know," said Allan. "That's civilized food, and pie crust is hard to digest—"

"Not my mother's!" interrupted Doug.

"Well, there would be plenty of wild apples where I would go," said Allan.

They were both silent again. Doug reached out and pulled a young dandelion leaf and began to nibble it.

"Don't eat that—it might be poisonous!" warned Allan.

"Dandelions poisonous? Don't be silly. They are healthy. Why, this dandelion leaf has twenty-five times more vitamin-A content than tomato juice, and fifty times more than that grass they call asparagus—"

"Is that right? I've heard of eating a lot of things, but never dandelions."

"Well, we were talking about living on a desert island, and what do you think we would live on?"

"Yeah, that's right, but we can't live on dandelions, can we?"

"Certainly not. But think of all the wild foods there are. Many of them just growing around everywhere and people not knowing they are good to eat. I'm just getting into that in Scouting. You'll learn about it soon. I know that a lot of attention is being given by the Army, Navy, and Air Force to teaching men to live off the land. Many men dropped behind the enemy lines without food have to know the very things they are teaching Scouts. They have to know what things to eat to keep them alive. The Navy prints a book on *How to Survive on Land and Sea,* and in the Scout *Handbook for Boys,* the *Explorer Manual,* and a little book on *Nature Adventuring* there are all kinds of wild foods listed. Anybody who knows about these

156

things can live like a king in the wilds."

"Yeah, I guess so."

And they continued daydreaming about living in the wilds far away from civilization. Scouts actually do this. They set out in Patrols, carrying the least possible equipment, to live on nature. They have fun and plenty of adventure.

They construct lean-tos as shelters for the night. They make their own fishing lines from fibers of bark or stalks. They make their fires by friction, using native materials for their fire-making sets. And they know enough about wild foods to find enough edible plants to make their meals complete.

The list of wild foods is a long one. There are many kinds of roots that make good eating. But most wild roots are bitter and usually have to be cooked in two sets of water. Arrowhead tubers can be eaten raw but taste better when boiled. Canadians cut up dandelion roots in their salads. The cattail root stocks and young shoots make good eating when boiled. There is the tuber of the Indian cucumber, which is good raw, with the flavor of the cultivated cucumber. Other roots include those of the groundnut, evening primrose, jack-in-the-pulpit, hog peanut, wild potato vine, bitter-root, prairie apple, and Jerusalem artichoke.

For greens, which have to be boiled, there are the dandelion, pokeweed shoots, milkweed shoots, lamb's-quarters, marsh marigold, curly dock, black mustard, and common plantain. "Fiddleheads" of young ferns are excellent. Wild rice is a delicacy.

There are many kinds of desserts. A few include the wild strawberry, red and black raspberry, wild grape, May apple (this is the American mandrake and its roots and leaves are poisonous), black walnut, hazelnut, piñon nut, and chestnut.

Beverages can be made from red stag-horn sumac fruits, sassafras bark, black birch twigs, New Jersey tea plant, spearmint, and Osage tea plant. Catnip also makes a good tea, and the French use it in cooking.

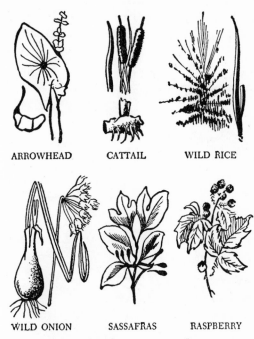

ARROWHEAD   CATTAIL   WILD RICE

WILD ONION   SASSAFRAS   RASPBERRY

Many wild plants are good to eat

Sugar and sirup can be obtained from the maple tree, chewing gum from spruce and pine gum.

There are many other things growing wild which can be eaten, among them the mushrooms. But only an expert can detect the poisonous from the edible, and the Scout plays safe and leaves these alone. See SURVIVAL TECHNIQUES.

Wildlife. The Scout tries to preserve and protect America's wildlife. Many Troops set up and maintain wildlife and bird sanctuaries. They set up shelters and feeding stations in the winter and keep them filled with food for birds and small animals. They plant trees and shrubs that produce food and shelter. They provide

157

Winter camping requires plenty of knowledge and skill

watering places in the summer. Many Scouts build nature trails to teach others about the kind of food and shelter that birds and animals need. They co-operate with local agencies, make exhibits for schools, give talks in schools and elsewhere about wildlife protection and conservation. See BALANCE OF NATURE, BIRD FEEDERS, CONSERVATION PLEDGE, JAMES E. WEST CONSERVATION SCHOLARSHIP, SCOUT OATH AND LAW, WOODLORE.

Window Display (Scout Week). During Scout Week, many Troops set up displays of Scout activities in store windows, with the permission of the owners. Camping scenes and handicraft items are the most popular. Sometimes Scouts give demonstrations of such things as fire by friction or other Scoutcraft skills in windows or in a public square out of doors.

Winter Camping. Nature seemed at rest, dug in for the winter. The boughs of the trees were heavy with snow, and the ground was blanketed in white. The birds had gone to a warmer climate. It was still and cold.

But from a clump of trees there came a sign of life. Smoke arose in a thin column. There was a smell of frying bacon. The rattle of a tin pot. A sharp axe biting into wood. The sound of merry voices.

Here, in this otherwise deserted and desolate spot, was a small camp of Scouts. Three snug tents were set up. One Scout was preparing breakfast, kneeling before the fire. Another was chopping wood. A third was bringing water.

In looking upon this scene one could see at once that the Scouts were thoroughly at home. They knew exactly what they were doing. They were warmly dressed. They had the proper equipment for keeping warm at night. They were having fun

and enjoying adventure.

Winter camping is a real he-man activity. It is the type of camping that requires plenty of wildwood knowledge. But when the winter camper has spunk and knows what he is doing, it is one of the most enjoyable types of camping.

The Scout divides his recipe for enjoyable winter camping into five divisions. One is the proper clothing—mostly of wool from the skin out, with a closely woven, water-repellent cotton jacket to keep out wind and rain. Wool stockings and wool socks, of course, with high-cut shoes a size or two larger than for ordinary wear.

For his shelter he may go to a log cabin. Or he may prefer a roomy tent, but one with an open front so that the warmth of a reflector fire can come in. A good bed is made on a frame filled with light brush, dead leaves, spruce or hemlock twigs, and covered with a ground sheet or tarpaulin. Four medium-weight blankets are better than two heavy ones.

And his food! Plenty of heat-producing foods—fats and sugars. Breakfast of hot cereal, griddlecakes, and bacon or sausage, with a good hot beverage. Lunch of pork and beans and a soup made from a dehydrated soup mix, served steaming hot! For supper he has a good, rich stew.

In his winter camp the Scout keeps busy. He staggers his activities during the day so that he will have plenty to occupy him, with rest periods in between. He likes skiing and tobogganing. Or snowball fights, skating, and treasure hunts. He likes to explore, too, and study nature. He breathes the clean, healthy air and he knows he never felt better in his life. See CAMPING (ADVENTURE), FIRE BUILDING, SHELTERS, TENTS.

Wolf. The second rank in Cub Scouting. See CUB SCOUT.

Wood Badge Training. A training course adapted from the famous Gilwell Wood Badge Course. The Wood Badge is a leather thong with two wooden beads, worn around the neck. Only selected Scout leaders may take the training which includes campcraft, camp cooking, first aid, games, pioneering, compass, and many other advanced Scouting skills. See GIL-WELL TRAINING CENTER.

Woodcraft. Skill in things that belong to woodland life.

Woodlore. The Scout might also refer to this as wood sense. It means a knowledge of a region's animals, rocks, minerals, people, history, topography, food possibilities, and climate. It means also how to adapt himself to live comfortably in the region. See SURVIVAL TECHNIQUES, WILD FOODS.

Woodsman's Tools. See AXE, KNIFE.

World Brotherhood of Scouting. "A Scout is friendly . . . a brother to every other Scout." This means every other Scout in the world, and there are over 5,000,000 Scouts. They wear the same basic type of uniform, with variations according to country and climate. They observe the same Scout Oath and Law. World Brotherhood in Scouting is best demonstrated at a World Jamboree. See JAMBOREE (WORLD), WORLD SCOUTING.

World Scouting. When a boy joins a Scout Troop—or other Unit—he becomes a part of a great worldwide movement. The same day he is on a hike, building a bridge, or meeting with his Patrol, Scouts in other countries of the world will be doing the same thing. For there are Scouts from Canada to the Argentine, from Iceland to Australia, and from Denmark to South Africa —over 5,000,000 of them.

Every four years thousands of Scouts of the world meet in one big camp at a World Jamboree. Here they have two weeks of real adventure and fellowship, showing one another their favorite games and how they camp back home.

They are helping to build good will among the nations of the world which some day may help bring universal peace. See INTERNATIONAL SCOUT BUREAU, JAMBOREE (WORLD), WORLD BROTHERHOOD OF SCOUTING.

Printed in U.S.A.